TIGER

TIGER

STEPHEN MILLS

FIREFLY BOOKS

A FIREFLY BOOK

Published by Firefly Books Ltd. 2004

First published 2004 by BBC Books, BBC Worldwide Ltd,
Woodlands, 80 Wood Lane, London W12 0TT

First printing

Publisher Cataloging-in-Publication Data (U.S.)
Mills, Stephen.
   Tiger / Stephen Mills. –1st ed.
[168] p. : col. photos. ;   cm.
Includes bibliographical references and index.
Summary: Discussion of tiger behavior including social structures, breeding patterns,
family life, eating habits and communication. Also addresses religious significance
of tigers, shrinking habitat, tiger attacks, conservation efforts and how and where
to observe tigers in the wild.
ISBN 1-55297-949-0 (pbk.)
1. Tigers. 2. Tigers — Behavior. I. Title.
599.756 21   QL737.C23.M555 2004

National Library of Canada Cataloguing in Publication
Mills, Stephen
        Tiger / Stephen Mills.
Includes bibliographical references and index.
ISBN 1-55297-949-0
        1. Tigers. I. Title.
QL737.C23M545 2004   599.756   C2003-907436-6

Published in the United States in 2004 by
Firefly Books (U.S.) Inc.
P.O. Box 1338, Ellicott Station
Buffalo, New York 14205

Published in Canada in 2004 by
Firefly Books Ltd.
66 Leek Crescent
Richmond Hill, Ontario L4B 1H1

Printed in Singapore

To my family and special friends
and a future for wild tigers

Contents

Introduction

One autumn night, deep in the Indian forests of Uttar Pradesh, I was woken by the huge roar of a tiger. It was so close it shook the air around me, filling the darkness with stark terror. I shone my torch out of my open cabin door and was astonished by what I saw. The compound of the deserted forest lodge where I was staying was filled with motionless jackals, 20 or more, petrified, stock-still. Behind them, the light reflected the 100 pin-point eyes of a mass of chital pressed against the perimeter fence, staring helplessly in at me. My companion and I crept to our jeep, drove it out of the camp and pointed the headlights into the forest. Then the strangest thing happened. One by one the chital turned from the fence and stepped into the light. Straight-legged with fright, they picked their way along the line of the beam towards us, treating it like a drawbridge let down to rescue them, knowing that where the light was no tiger could be. Eyes wide, they tiptoed up onto the road, each one inching past us, as close as it dared, brushing the car. Then they were gone, released from terror, bouncing into the comfortable jungle behind us. We sat in silence, watching the empty carpet of light, but nothing else ventured onto it. We never saw the tiger yet that transfixing of the jungle by its invisible force was somehow more potent than if the animal had merely appeared.

Those of us who are blessed with an unquestioning lifelong love of nature are moved by all forms of life. Nevertheless, most of us would confess to some special passion. For me there are three, perhaps four, wildlife experiences that rise above all others: a solitary, distant polar bear, a white dot in a white world, patrolling the empty Arctic ice-cap; a great whale breaching the surface of the ocean; the howling of wolves in a Scandinavian autumn; and a tiger. And of all these, the tiger remains the most profound. I have had hundreds and hundreds of tiger sightings. I can remember them all. Even now, after so many years, I love to share the excitement of someone else's first tiger. Tigers are quite simply the most beautiful animal on earth. They are so amazingly orange, so bright, sometimes so surprisingly invisible. The white spots on their black furry ears are so endearing. They have giant paws like teddy bears, their tails are so expressive, their amber eyes so changeable and they are so big. The largest male on record was 3.25m (10 feet 7 inches) from nose to tail. A male can weigh 225-270 kg (500–600 lb), a female 100–175 kg (220–385 lb). Occasionally, when you see one padding close by through the forest, it can suddenly seem too large for the landscape, like some relic from a more expansive age. Knowing all this I am not sure I would want to live in a world that no longer contained wild tigers.

The modern tiger was never found in Africa. It is strictly an Asian species, having evolved some two million years ago, probably in what is now northern China. Tigers first appeared in human art on 5000-year-old seals from the Harappan civilization of the Indus Valley and it is not surprising that in the spiritual lands of Asia they have acquired a religious significance and supernatural potency. In India the tiger is the hallowed steed of the Hindu Goddess Durga and is thought of as a god in its own right. In Tibet lamas believe it has the power to avert evil. In China the markings on a tiger's head are thought to spell the pictogram 'wang' or 'king' and children are still given caps and pillows in the shape of tigers to give them vigour. In Sumatra, where the tiger seems to be peculiarly benign, traditional people do not mention its name, merely referring to it reverentially as 'our friend'. The most moving testament to the respect in which tigers are held emerged in an Indian documentary film by the Bedi brothers. It showed a procession in which the body of a man-eating tiger was carried through the villages that it had persecuted. This was not, however, a demonstration of vulgar triumph but rather of sadness and reverence. The villagers strewed the tiger with flowers and, in a deeply eloquent gesture, one lady who had herself been mauled, gently touched the tiger's paw.

How does a tiger stalk its prey?
What is the real purpose of alarm calls?
How often does a tiger fail in a chase or ambush?
What factors make a hunt successful?
What is the value of a deep knowledge of its landscape to a hunter like the tiger?

The Tiger as Hunter
What Makes a Successful Predator?

Early one November morning in 2000 I was in the Kanha meadows in the Indian state of Madhya Pradesh, straining for a sight of a hunting tigress. The mist was still clinging in wisps to the tips of the elephant grass and a single tree-pie was fluting from the trees behind us but the chital that had drawn us there had stopped calling. We were on the edge of a broad clearing in the forest – a sea of long grass stretching away to distant wooded shores. In front of us a family of wild boar were rooting their way busily among the grass stems, and away to our right three barasingha hinds were watching us with fading interest. It was our forest guard, standing precariously on tiptoe on the roll bar of the jeep, who spotted the tigress. For a brief second he saw just her tail. She was 1 km (½ mile) away, far over to our left, creeping from left to right. Soon there were four of us perched like cormorants on the creaky excrescences of the jeep.

The barasingha (swamp deer) now seemed to be feeding, their heads dipping down beneath the horizon of grass heads. Ten minutes later I saw the tigress – again for half a second – side-on as she passed between bushes, now hundreds of metres to the right of our first glimpse. It was another 15 minutes before we saw her again. Her head came up like a periscope about 50 m (160 feet) from the deer – visible to us from our vantage point but not yet to them. She had inched her way in a wide semicircle so that she could approach them downwind without alerting them; now all she had to do was worm herself in close enough for a charge. She disappeared, while we fixed our binoculars on the dense grass between her and the deer and held our breath. We waited. More minutes passed. The tree-pie had stopped calling. Then suddenly it was all over. The three deer looked up, ears stretched, peering into the grass ahead of them. One of them

stamped her foot and barked, a loud, creaky call, her breath steaming round her mouth. The other two called and there was the tigress, having materialized once more, close but not quite close enough, staring at them while they stared at her. They all knew that she had failed and, with a great swish of her tail, the frustrated tigress bounded into a nearby bush and the deer picked their way slowly to safer grazing.

The tigress had probably spent the best part of an hour traversing the meadow, remaining almost entirely invisible and yet, after all that effort, she had had to abandon the hunt. I saw the same tigress give up another attempt in almost the same place a couple of days later – she was easily recognized because she had a faint dark circle instead of a stripe on each of her hips. This time she crept several hundred metres onto two chital (spotted deer), but again the deer saw her at the last minute and the whole character of her body changed. One moment she was tense with concentration, oozing forward through the dry, crackly grass in absolute silence; the next she was turning away stiff-legged and scuffing the leaves and grass stems noisily. Having

Below: The tiger's stripes merge with the shadows and the foliage to make it almost invisible.

been caught out like a child playing Grandma's Footsteps, it was as if she was literally stamping her feet in irritation.

Such frustrations are a normal part of a tiger's working week. The vast majority of hunts fail. Admittedly, a tiger is well equipped for its work. If it were not a supreme hunter, the species would already be extinct. It has the strength and burst of speed over a short distance to kill almost anything in the jungle but perhaps its most essential skill is its stalking ability. A tiger can move with absolute silence. I remember sitting in an open jeep one night in Kishanpur in Uttar Pradesh waiting for a tiger that I had glimpsed coming my way up a forest track. The jungle was very quiet and I was straining my ears for the sound of a footfall, of breathing, of any sign of the tiger's approach. There was a thin pool of moonlight bathing the path just in front of the jeep. Suddenly, in a heartbeat, it filled with tiger, although I never heard a sound. The tiger stood looking in at me, then glided noiselessly away, the soft pads of its feet sucking the sound of its steps into themselves.

Tigers are so supple that they can squeeze into the most untigerlike spaces. I once watched the Kanha tigress trying to

avoid being spotted by a couple of tourist jeeps. To reach dense cover she had to cross open ground, with only a rib of short stubble connecting the bush in which she was hiding to her destination, so she flattened herself on her belly and squirmed like an eel through the spiky grass stems. The movement of her body was almost liquid and only her head and her angled shoulder blades gave her any depth at all. It was like seeing a tiger flow.

Finally, of course, there is the tiger's astonishing camouflage: stripes that disappear among crosshatched grass stems and dappled forest understorey. Even though it is a huge animal, a tiger on the move can be all but impossible to see. One lying in ambush is truly invisible. And the speed of its first leap can be electrifying. In April 2003 I saw an elephant get too close to a tigress asleep in a pool. In less than the blink of an eye, the tigress 'disappeared' and rematerialized 10 m (33 feet) away. Yet the odds in any individual hunt are stacked against the tiger's success. For one thing, there are so many eyes marking its progress. The orchestra of alarm calls contains many instruments, from the screeching of lapwings and peacocks, through the gruff

coughing of langur monkeys and the appealing cries of chital to the deep, roaring bark of sambar deer. The real purpose of these alarms is, I suspect, more to inform the predator that he has been rumbled than deliberately to warn other prey species in the forest of the danger. When a deer sees a tiger it may even walk towards it rather than away, calling conspicuously. The tiger then knows he has lost the advantage of surprise and almost always gives up the stalk. Giving the alarm call makes you the safest deer in the jungle at that moment. Members of your family group benefit directly from your alertness but I have sometimes observed that other deer in nearby groups may take no notice unless they see or smell the tiger for themselves and that alarms are not always passed on from one set of animals to another. Much has been written about the so-called 'symbiotic' relationship between chital and langurs (and, in Africa, between baboons and impala). The monkeys are said to benefit from the chitals' excellent noses and the chital have the monkeys up trees as lookouts. It is true that the two species are often together but the degree to which they really share information has been little tested. Monkeys are messy eaters. They drop lots of fresh young leaves from the upper canopy that the deer could never reach for themselves and I believe their relationship owes more to this mundane fact than to any mutual warning mechanism.

Whatever the case, there is no doubt that the barrage of alarm calls a tiger is likely to provoke does not make its job any easier and it can be a real challenge to evade the acute defensive radar of its prey. Monkeys are rarely caught because they can run up trees, which a tiger cannot. Peacocks and jungle fowl can fly, and the ungulates (hoofed animals) that tigers like best are all extremely alert. They also live in groups or herds and either defend each other, as gaur may, or at least alert each other. And when they flee they explode away at enormous speed. It is perhaps not surprising then that a tiger rarely gets close enough to its prey to charge and that even when it does it usually misses.

Valmik Thapar, for instance, who has been studying the tigers of Ranthambhore National Park in Rajasthan for nearly 30 years, records an incident there in November 1982 when a tigress he called Nick Ear missed a large sambar stag that was less than 2 m (6½ feet) from her. She leapt out of a bush at it but was a bit slow and clumsy – perhaps because she had been snoozing – and the deer jumped out of the way.

Success or failure?

Most observers agree that a tiger's success rate is low: somewhere between one in ten attempts and one in 20. George Schaller, who made the first truly scientific study of wild tigers in Kanha in the 1960s, reported a figure of 12 misses to one hit, while Valmik Thapar and Fateh Singh Rathore (formerly field director of Ranthambhore) estimated a 10 per cent scoring rate; but, as tiger ecologist Dr Ullas Karanth says, this is mostly guesswork. We don't witness most of the night hunts, and during the daytime we have to factor in the influence of our own presence as observers. Do we distract the predator so that it has to keep an eye on us while it is hunting? Do we distract the prey so that it is watching us rather than the tiger? Do we, on the other hand, make the prey generally more alert and so disadvantage the tiger? Or does the tiger ever exploit us, using our vehicles, for instance, to hide its approach? The answer is that probably all these elements come into play at different times. Whatever the precise truth, most of the hunting efforts that are witnessed are unsuccessful, and the ratio for tigers is comparable to that of lions in Africa. Lions have the advantage of working together but they often hunt in more

Previous page: Tiger disembowelling its prey.
Right: After killing its prey a tiger usually drags it by its head to a safe place for eating.

open ground where they are more easily seen. Tigers must hunt alone and their prey is more dispersed but they have good cover for stalking. The pros and cons seem to balance each other out. The strike rate for most predators, including birds of prey, seems to be quite low. So what turns a statistical improbability into a hit? Why, one in ten or one in 20 times, does a tiger get lucky?

In December 1999 I was in Kanha. It was late afternoon towards the end of a game drive and we were returning to the Kisili Gate to leave the park. In the last of the sunshine a big group of wild boar was feeding. There were at least 30 of them, big males, females, adolescents and youngsters, some half hidden

by dense, low tussocks. Behind them was a grass bank and off to the left a wide patch of longer grass with what looked like the round top of a post sticking up out of it. My eye went back to the boars, then back to the post. Through binoculars it wasn't a post, it was the head of a small tigress, keeping very still. She must have been craning her neck, like a serval cat, because the grass was a metre or so high and her head was all that was visible. She was at least 150 m (500 feet) from the boars and from her angle it was not clear that she could even see them. After a minute, however, the head disappeared. The next time I saw the post it was 50 m (160 feet) closer to the boars. Then it was gone again, to reappear about 60 m (195 feet) from them, at which point she broke into a series of great bounds, springing like a hurdler over the tops of the grass. When she broke cover, the wild boar exploded in all directions, but she headed right for the thickest tussocks at the heart of the group, running in on top of a young pig that seemed to get caught up in the grass. There was a terrible squealing, then silence, and only the slope of her back could be seen as she crouched over her meal.

If you'd asked me to place bets before the hunt began, I would have laid good money on it that she would not succeed. She started her charge from too far away, she had to struggle through the long grass before she could get up speed and there were lots of piggy eyes and ears on the watch. She may just have been lucky or she may have assessed the boars' escape routes, reckoning that they might be delayed by the bank behind them or get tangled in the tussocks – which is after all what happened. She did not let herself be deflected by the scattering pigs, but kept her eye on one victim. Was it carrying an injury or feeling under the weather and had she spotted this when she was being a

Left and opposite: A tiger needs to stalk its prey, relying on surprise and a quick dash at the end.

fence post? We can only guess but the probability is that she had a basic strategy in mind when she decided to charge.

Unfortunately, we still do not know all there is to know about what makes a tiger's hunt successful. Not many people have seen tigers kill in the wild and very few observers have seen numerous tigers kill numerous times. Schaller saw only one successful hunt in his time in Kanha and until the last 20 years the vast majority of witnessed kills involved domestic livestock, usually tethered as bait. The evidence, however, suggests that, while some kills are pure serendipity, in most cases tigers don't make random attacks. They think on their feet.

The Irish cameraman Colin Stafford Johnson made an interesting observation when he was filming for a BBC programme (*Danger in Tiger Paradise*) in Ranthambhore in 2001. He and his driver Salim Ali were following a five-year-old male they had called Chips. The tiger was actually behind their jeep when it noticed a large chital stag up ahead. The deer jumped up onto the road about 50 m (160 feet) ahead, just at a point where further escape to the sides was blocked by a steep embankment. Chips immediately charged, passing so close to the jeep that his tail swiped across Salim Ali's face! Deer and tiger disappeared round a bend in the road. Perhaps the deer stopped for a moment to

check whether he'd shaken off the tiger. If so, he made a fatal mistake because Chips was right behind him and caught him. The tiger had covered at least 275 m (900 feet) flat out. In fact he was so tired that he just toppled the deer and lay on top of it for five minutes until he recovered his strength. Then he throttled it.

It's extremely rare for a mature (therefore experienced) tiger to try to outpace a deer in an open race. Tigers are not like cheetahs. They are not built for long high-speed chases and, in the normal course of events, the deer will twist and turn with sufficient agility to elude any tiger. But this was not a normal event. In this case the deer could only run in one direction. The question is: did the tiger know this and is this why he sustained the chase? Did he know that all he had to do was keep on running and that eventually he would catch the deer – that, for sheer power, he held the winning hand?

A study on wolves in Scandinavia may throw some incidental light on this. Researcher Camilla Wikenros looked at the hunting success of a small wolf pack chasing moose and roe deer in the province of Dalarna in south central Sweden during the winters of 1999 and 2000. She found that the average chase was quite short – around 75–80 m (245–260 feet) if the prey was a moose and 150 m (500 feet) for roe deer – and that these lengths did not vary much whether the chase was successful or abandoned. On two occasions, however, she tracked successful moose kills that had lasted 800 and 900 m (2600 and 2950 feet) respectively and a successful roe kill that had involved a chase of over 1100 m (3600 feet). It would appear from these observations that when the wolves were convinced they would eventually win the race – and the critical factor was often snow depth – they were willing to stretch a chase to an exhausting length up to ten times their usual effort. Confidence, it seems, makes all the difference. Indeed, this is borne out by the fact that the wolves were generally willing to chase roe deer further than moose, on the basis that if they had not caught a moose (which is huge in comparison) within a short distance, they might not have the strength left to bring it down even if they caught up with it.

Survival of the most sensible

The implication is that a predator will continue a chase not because it is stupid and stubborn, or instinctively programmed never to give up, but because it believes it will be successful. It will be making continuous calculations as to whether it is gaining or not and it will give up as soon as it thinks it is wasting its energy. In other words, it is thinking. The probability is that Chips realized the deer could not escape to right or left and that's why he went hammering on. If, however, he did that every time he saw a deer, he would blow a fuse. This ability to weigh correctly the chances of success is crucial to a predator. A deer can run to a standstill and, if the danger passes, can immediately stuff itself with food ready for the next chase. But an exhausted, unsuccessful tiger cannot recover so easily. In fact, it could run itself out of a living.

Of course there are exceptions. In November 1998 I watched a cheetah race across several kilometres of the rolling plains of Lobo in the Serengeti in pursuit of a huge herd of adult wildebeest. My companions thought the incident was interesting because they were seeing a cheetah at full speed – and that was true – but what was really surprising was that it had no hope of catching anything. Perhaps it was a particularly exuberant character that hadn't read the manual, or a foolish youngster without the experience to know when to stop. Or could it have been a crafty individual testing the prey for signs of injury? In any case, even a cheetah could not make a habit of such extravagant expenditure of energy. For predators, and especially tigers, the rule is not merely 'survival of the fittest' but survival of the most sensible.

This is why many people who have witnessed wild tigers making a kill have been struck by how mundane the final action can be. Firstly, it is silent. Tigers do not roar or growl or snarl when they are planning to kill something. They concentrate. And they like to get close. Tigers rarely launch an attack from a distance much greater than 10–20 m (33–60 feet), relying on their lightning spring and usually giving up if they think they have been spotted. If they keep the all-important element of surprise, then typically they make a few sudden bounds, reach out and pull the victim down, then either bite it at the back of the neck or through the skull or hold its throat until it is dead. That's it. The only sound I have sometimes heard is the disconcerting gagging of a strangled deer. Sometimes so little happens that it looks as if the tiger is just helping itself from the supermarket shelves. Indeed, some observers have commented that the prey even stood still, 'as if it knew its fate'. In nature the moment of predation is frequently like that. I have seen a cheetah in the Serengeti strolling along and then nonchalantly turning its head to pick up a crouching hare from the grass – a hare that could have bolted and perhaps made a successful dash for it but instead made the fateful error – this time – of sitting still and hoping not to be seen. I don't think the victim knows its fate, I think it simply hesitates. It makes the wrong decision. In the moment of choice the scales are tipped. So Chips made the right choice to continue chasing the deer on the road. The deer made the wrong choice if it stopped to look back.

In the UK, traditional natural history lore had it that large rabbits were mesmerized by small deadly stoats and that's why they let themselves be caught. I was told this myself as a boy by the local gamekeeper near my parents' home in Oxfordshire. But when later, in Ireland, I watched a stoat hunting a rabbit, I saw something different happening. The rabbit was not mesmerized, because it did not seem to know it was being hunted. It would see the stoat, bounce off for 10 m (33 feet) or so and then sit down. It sat down more and more frequently because, I think, it was lost. Rabbits operate mostly within 50 m (160 feet) of their burrows. The stoat had pushed it beyond its familiar landmarks so it was stopping to have a think. Poor old rabbit!

The killing fields

Success either in escaping a predator or in catching prey has a lot to do with confidence. A tentative rabbit gets caught. A hesitant tiger misses its mark. Familiarity with the landscape is a great confidence-booster. The deer was caught because it didn't know how to get off the road. The rabbit couldn't find its way back to its burrow. For a hunter, intimate knowledge of the lie of the land is like an extra tool. A tiger safe within its home range is often a creature of habit. It has its favourite paths. It knows how to use the dried streambeds that allow it to creep noiselessly and invisibly. It knows the slopes and folds of land that will hide its approach or give it the benefit of a downward rush on its prey – one of the easiest kills I have witnessed involved little more than a hop and a skip down from a stony incline onto a deer that was not looking up. The tiger knows where its prey is likely to be and is acutely aware of their patterns of movement. It will repeat successful hunting tactics over and over again.

This conscripting of the landscape into the arsenal of hunting equipment is common to most predators. I have spent many hours over 15 years looking out of my favourite window in southwest Ireland. The view shows me rolling slopes of rough pasture and patches of submaritime heath with the Atlantic Ocean beyond. There is a particular tufty hillock covered with thyme and wind-pruned heather that I call the 'killing field'. It is rich in ants, moth larvae and grasshoppers, so there are always a couple of meadow pipits or skylarks feeding there. The local sparrowhawk seems to know this. From my vantage point I see it, or its progeny, hundreds of metres away, hurtling at top speed just above the ground, like a fighter bomber, hugging the folds of the land for meadow pipit radar silence until suddenly it is up over

the hillock and it plucks the panicked pipit at the moment of lift-off. I have seen this too often to be coincidence. The sparrowhawk is clearly using the landscape for surprise, knowing that when it tops the best pipit feeding ground it will be travelling much too fast for its prey to outpace him.

Having a well-tried 'killing field' on one's home range must be very valuable to predators so it is not surprising that they hang on to them tenaciously. An extreme example of such habituated hunting behaviour was exhibited by the last pair of golden eagles to breed in Ireland. Between 1953 and 1960 they bred on the northeast coast of County Antrim but when a researcher examined their nest he found the remains of Scottish blue hares. These are not found in Ireland, which has its own endemic subspecies, so it would appear that the eagles were commuting to Scotland to catch their prey. They were flapping off over the sea to the Mull of Kintyre 20 km (12 miles) away, where they had been born, to do their hunting over familiar terrain,

presumably under the impression that the sea was just a big lake and quite unaware that they were making ornithological history by crossing national boundaries.

The survival value of a familiar hunting landscape must be at least as high for a tiger as for an eagle. Hunting as it does mostly alone, and pursuing prey that is rarely numerous, a tiger needs all the help it can get from strategic rocks, river beds, bushes and other hiding places. So hunting rights are likely to be one of the resources that a tiger defends when it chases another tiger off its home range. We have some indirect evidence for this in the way tigers treat leopards. On the whole tigers don't like leopards. They chase them up trees and will kill and even eat them. Yet they appear to be more tolerant of them in areas where they don't have to compete with them for food. Leopards are much smaller than tigers. Even a big male rarely exceeds 100 kg (220 lb), so in an ideal world leopards concentrate on smaller prey – from peacocks, monkeys and small deer like muntjak up to chital – while tigers

start at chital and munch their way up through sambar to gaur (a type of wild ox). But in many areas, like the meadows of Kanha in Madhya Pradesh and Chitwan in Nepal, both species go for chital because they are the most abundant prey. The result, researchers have found, is that in both places tigers exclude leopards from the best hunting grounds. In Nagarahole in Karnataka, however, Ullas Karanth has discovered a different pattern. There large prey, like gaur, are more common than elsewhere and, because tigers prefer the economic advantage of killing big animals when they are available, they don't regard the leopards as such serious competition. Consequently, leopards are common in the heart of the Nagarahole forests.

Of course, there are other reasons why a resident tiger may be aggressive to an intruder tiger – defence of mating privileges, for example – but as far as food is concerned, what applies to leopards presumably applies to other tigers as well.

Exclusion from the familiar hunting grounds probably contributes to the high level of mortality among young male tigers after they have left home. Ullas Karanth gives the annual estimated mortality rate of 'transient' tigers as 30–35 per cent per year and states that most perish before reaching full maturity. The majority of these doomed transients are male. They have much to contend with and often end up on the fringes of reserves, where they face starvation (see *Family Life: Growing Up* chapter). It is usually assumed that they go hungry because there is no food for them – or they are forced to kill livestock and may be poisoned by villagers. This is undoubtedly true but the fact that a tiger is young, inexperienced and trying to find its way round a strange environment whose features don't help it must be a major factor.

One of the most famous cases of a tiger perfecting its use of the landscape to create its own 'killing field' is described by Valmik Thapar in his excellent book *Tiger: Portrait of a Predator*. He called the tiger Genghis because he was so big and confident and such an effective killer. Genghis, says Thapar, was 'an innovator'. He lived in the early to mid-1980s in Ranthambhore National Park where he taught himself how to make water work for him. At the centre of the park are several large lakes, each with a short grass margin and a strip of long grass beyond. Genghis used the long grass, as any tiger would, for stalking sambar that were feeding in and around the water. When he was close enough, he would break cover and charge at full tilt, hoping either to squeeze the deer against the lakeside and catch them as they turned or to panic them so that they ran back into the water – discovering too late to their cost that wading slowed them down. But then he refined his technique. He found he could startle them and then run 'like a cheetah' 150 m (500 feet) across open grazing to cut them off at one or other corner of the lake. Finally, he realized he could build up such momentum as he came to the lake edge that he could just swim out and take the sambar even before they were out of the water. Genghis was definitely a creature of habit. Apparently he had one favourite bush, 'like a graveyard', where he dragged many of his victims. So predictable did he become in 1984 that between March and May observers witnessed him make no fewer than 18 kills.

Genghis disappeared – possibly having been poached – in October 1984 but apparently he bequeathed his tricks to one of his mates, a tigress called Noon. She practised them with energy, though slightly less skill, and the technique was recorded by Stanley Breedon and Belinda Wright in a beautiful film called *Land of the Tiger*. I never saw Genghis or Noon. I have only seen the footage and the photographs, though even through these second-hand media it is clear just how spectacular those tigers were.

Opposite: Some of the tigers at Ranthambhore have learned to use the lake as part of their hunting technique, trapping prey close to or even in the water.

What do tigers like best?

Does a tiger's prey ever fight back?

What are the most surprising things that tigers eat?

Can tigers kill rhinos and elephants?

How do we study the tiger's diet?

Does prey vary from region to region?

How much does a tiger eat?

The Tiger's Prey
Love Thy Ungulate

Spectacular hunts are not the norm. A hunting tiger is not interested in impressing an audience. Its priorities are simple: to catch the biggest dinner it can find, as easily as possible with the minimum expenditure of energy and the smallest risk of injury to itself. At first sight, this is hardly a recipe for heroism but, as we shall see, a tiger's life is tough enough. It doesn't need histrionics before every meal. In any case, to take most prey requires more skill than is immediately obvious. Scientist John Seidensticker describes this well when he says that a 'tiger, like a martial arts master, uses the prey's own motion to bring it down', never committing itself, 'to a movement until after the prey does'.

Tigers are immensely strong. In his seminal book *The Deer and the Tiger* George Schaller reported a tigress that had carried the '142 pound [65 kg] forequarters of a cow 600 feet [180 m] along a stream bed and 100 feet [30 m] up into a mass of boulders without leaving a drag mark' and he quotes E. A. Smythies' observation of a tiger that had jumped 4.5 m (15 feet) up a stream bank with a 68-kg (150-lb) carcass in its mouth. Tigers almost always move their kills, dragging them sometimes for hundreds of metres until they find safe cover in which to hide them. Schaller's record was a tigress that dragged a chital 550 m (1800 feet). Nevertheless, a tiger rarely kills by strength alone. It doesn't pick up a 250-kg (550-lb) sambar stag and knock its head on a rock; it pulls it down, letting gravity help. Ullas Karanth has shown that tigers in Nagarahole actually prefer to kill gaur, which can weigh up to 1000 kg (2200 lb) – four times the weight of a big tiger. To tackle such a huge animal and avoid any sporting injury to oneself requires immense skill.

My friend the late S. Deb Roy, who ended his distinguished career as Deputy Inspector General of Forests (Wildlife), told me an interesting story of a battle between a tiger and a huge bull buffalo. Deb Roy was for some years field director of Manas National Park, a Project Tiger reserve in Assam. Manas is one of the last refuges for truly wild buffalo, which can be formidable. One morning he came upon the signs of a gargantuan struggle that the tiger had clearly lost, for there it was, in the middle of a wide patch of battered grass, trampled flat like a striped carpet. The buffalo was not far away. It was in a wallow hole with just its nose showing. It spent every day for three months in that hole.

At night it would haul itself out and feed along the bank and Deb Roy could see that it had sustained terrible injuries. Nevertheless, the healing power of the mud and the animal's own strength helped it to recover and it lived on for two more years. The tiger, even if it had escaped, would not have survived because such injuries would have prevented it from hunting.

In that case what probably happened is that the tiger made a mistake at the moment of attack. Perhaps the buffalo saw it too soon or the tiger slipped as it went to throw itself and then found itself fighting not for dinner but for its own life. Tigers don't very often make mistakes. They prefer to abort a charge if they think they will have trouble. Most of the animals they hunt are armed. A sambar stag has a fierce set of swords in the form of antlers most of the year and so does a male chital. Wild boar have been known to kill leopards, but one of the most surprising threats comes from an unlikely source – the porcupine. Porcupines are probably rather tasty. They eat roots and lots of fruit, weigh 12–16 kg (26–35 lb) and a big male can be nearly 1 m (3¼ feet) long, so they make a good snack for a tiger. The problem is their quills. Tigers usually attack from the side and rear rather than from the front. This avoids head-on collisions with the hard, pointed bits of gaur, sambar, chital, barasingha, muntjak, hog deer and wild boar. It's not a good line of approach, however, for porcupines. They defend themselves not by 'firing' their quills but by scuttling backwards and embedding them in the enemy. To deal with this all a tiger has to do is come from the front and thwack the porcupine on the head but young tigers often don't know this and have to learn the hard way. Most researchers have had experience of a tiger temporarily crippled by a porcupine quill. Being very supple, tigers can usually pull these out but if the quill enters deep under the forearm the tiger cannot reach it and is likely to die of blood poisoning.

Opposite: Tigers kill their prey by a bite to the neck.

Strange meat

As a general rule, tigers are sensible, cautious and skilful hunters but they are also individuals and some can be unpredictable, even reckless. Nothing in the jungle is absolutely safe from attack. One morning in a patch of forest south of Dudhwa in Uttar Pradesh my assistant Druv Singh and I found evidence of a fight between a tigress and a python. For 20 m (65 feet) or so, the loose sand on the track was scooped into ridges by the flailing of a large snake and on either side were hollows and scrapes where the tiger had thrust for purchase. They seemed to have rolled off the track but further on the tigress's footprints rejoined it and padded calmly into the distance. We searched the scanty undergrowth for the snake and after half an hour or so we found it 50 m (160 feet) from the battlefield. It was, or had been, a very big python – 6 m (20 feet) long. Pythons that big are as rare as tigers and so, from a conservation point of view, it was a tragedy that the two had clashed. The snake's head was partly crushed but it was still alive, even though the tigress had eaten half a metre (1¾ feet) of its tail, taken a scallop out halfway along its back and eaten another chunk from the back of its head. We pulled some loose brushwood across so that it could not be spotted by vultures but, even though snakes have astonishing powers of recovery, I doubt that it survived. What puzzled us was why the tigress would have risked such a fierce fight for such a meagre meal. There have been anecdotal reports of leopards ripping open pythons that have just swallowed prey in order to eat the second-hand meal inside but our python had not been eviscerated. Since a big python is capable of taking a chital, it may be that the tigress treated the snake as a competitor. Or she may simply have had a taste for snakes and have been disturbed before she could finish her meal, since forest officers reported having witnessed the end of the encounter.

Individual tigers can be quirky. David Smith, a leading member of the Smithsonian Tiger Ecology Project, told me about

one in Chitwan that had a sideline speciality in sloth bears. Sloth bears are not at all slothful when disturbed. They move very fast and, if they feel cornered, they can turn on their attacker with devastating aggression. Up on their hind legs they are as tall as a man and their claws are as long as fingers and very powerful. I remember when Dr Anup Joshi was beginning his doctoral research and was radio-collaring them in Chitwan seeing one that had almost ripped its way out of a metal barrel-trap. Most tigers give sloth bears a wide berth. Bears do have one weakness, however. They adore termites – indeed, it is fascinating from an evolutionary point of view that there are so many termites so widely spread in India that they can actually provide a niche for such a big carnivore. And how clever the bears were to spot this, because they have no competitors. When they find an active termite mound they start digging and blowing and sucking and sending their long sinuous tongues down the underground passages, hoovering up the eggs and ants. This is an absorbing pastime. Smith's tiger seems to have noticed this. It used to creep up behind the feeding bear, wallop it on the back with all its might and then jump out of the way. The poor bear would apparently whirl in helpless circles like a broken-backed dervish until it was exhausted and the tiger could safely dispatch it.

During eight months of filming rhinos in Kaziranga in Assam over two years I came across three rhino calves that had been killed by tigers. The freshest kill I examined had a broken leg and puncture marks through the skull. The tiger, however, had not had the chance to feed and was probably chased off by the apoplectic mother. The more knowledgeable forest officers told me that they reckoned one in 50 calves might be taken by tigers and, while there was supposed to be a good density of tigers in the park and plenty of baby rhinos, there was no evidence of a tiger ever

Opposite: A tiger can kill almost anything it meets in the jungle, here an enormous python.

making a habit of rhino poaching. In his book *Unicornis, the Great Indian One-Horned Rhinoceros* Arup Kumar Dutta has a fanciful account of how tigers kill rhinos. 'Two tigers, a male and a female, usually stalk a rhino calf. While one tiger draws the mother away, its partner snatches the baby.' If this has ever happened, it must be very unusual since there are very few records of tigers hunting successfully as a team. He goes on to say 'when it is very young, the calf is loath to get in to wallow, and the mother often leaves it on the banks for a short while. Tigers take such opportunities to attack the baby.' This is not quite correct. Baby rhinos adore the water. I have filmed one accompanying its mother to the wallow within a few days of its birth. The truth is that nearly all female rhinos are terrifyingly protective of their calves. I know because on several occasions I have nearly been killed by them. They move appallingly fast and are equally protective of a dead calf. The mother of the baby whose skull had been punctured nearly overturned our vehicle when we first found her. For five days she hardly left the spot. Even two weeks later she was still returning every morning to chase the vultures away from the four little hooves that by then were all that was left of it. I have rarely been so frightened as I was trying to film her in an area that offered me no cover. A tiger tackles an accompanied calf at its peril. Rhino calves are more likely to be taken because they have become temporarily separated from their mothers. This can happen if another rhino chases her, if she is disturbed by poachers or intruders or occasionally during a heavy storm. There must, however, be the occasional careless mother who takes her eyes off her youngster and may well lose it to an opportunistic tiger.

The famous hunter and naturalist Jim Corbett reported seeing two tigers kill an elephant. Domesticated elephants are often nervous of tigers, which will occasionally attack them if they feel cornered. When we were filming in Bardia, in western Nepal, one of our elephants stepped into a bush where a tiger was hiding. The tiger roared and lashed out under the elephant's belly and the poor old elephant reared up on its hind legs like a circus pony. The tiger did not, however, hang around to dispute matters and no blood was drawn. One of the managers at Tiger Tops in Chitwan told me that her elephant had disturbed a tiger and then bolted but the enraged tiger had, for some reason, jumped on its back. All she had to hang on to was the rope that attached her cushion to the elephant and right behind her were the snarling jaws of a demented tiger. The tiger apparently clung on for over 100 m (320 feet). However, stories of tiger–elephant encounters

are a little like fishermen's tales – they gain something in the telling, and aggression between the two species in the wild is probably very rare. Elephant calves are usually protected at the heart of an alert herd but, like young rhinos, if for some reason they get separated from their relatives, a tiger can kill them.

Snakes, rhinos, elephants and bears are not standard fare for tigers – though admittedly, in his 1962 study in the Russian Far East, V. Abramov found that brown bears made up 8.4 per cent of the local tiger diet and researchers there have recently recorded the first case of a tiger killing a seal. The truth is that a hungry tiger will probably try anything once. Schaller analyzed the contents of 335 faeces collected in Kanha in 1964 and found eggshells, frog remains, winged termites and *Zizyphus* berries – each of them in just one different dropping. More interesting,

Below: Even one-horned rhino are vulnerable – tigers do kill small calves if mothers take their eyes off them.
Opposite: Tigers' tongues are so dry and rough that they can lick the fur off their prey.

perhaps, 13 of his samples contained nothing but 'fine black micaceous soil' – and these droppings mysteriously occurred only between 29 October and 23 December. What did this seasonal taste for earth imply? No one knows. Eight other faeces consisted entirely of grass. Grass is probably eaten by carnivores as a sort of scour. Dogs and wolves eat mouthfuls regularly. Perhaps the earth is a similar aid to digestion. I have occasionally required similar ballast myself in India. Meanwhile, Valmik Thapar quotes the hunter Frank Simpson who, in his 1886 book *Sport in Eastern Bengal*, wrote that he had 'once killed a tiger whose paunch was crammed full of grasshoppers or locusts'.

What the tiger likes best

The analysis of faeces is probably the most complete way of studying a tiger's diet. If faeces are collected across the entire spread of habitats within a tiger's range they provide an impartial window into the tiger's preferences. Sifting them carefully and examining them under the microscope may seem a bit ghoulish but it enables the scientist to identify almost everything the tiger has eaten. An observer rarely sees a tiger actually kill its prey, will never find all the carcasses of proven tiger kills before they rot away and may never even spot a tiger enjoying its occasional hors d'oeuvre of frogs' legs or termites. In the faeces, however, all is revealed. Nevertheless, although tigers may fill in the gaps between meals with all sorts of odd titbits, it would be quite wrong to think of them as omnivores. They are carnivores. Indeed, theirs is a highly specialized diet consisting overwhelmingly of one type of prey: ungulates – that is, animals with hooves; 52.2 per cent of Schaller's sampled faeces in Kanha contained just one species, chital. Not surprisingly, this was the most numerous larger ungulate in his study area. In Nagarahole, Ullas Karanth found that five species (gaur, sambar, chital, muntjak and wild pig) comprised over 95 per cent of the meat devoured in the park.

Wherever the tiger's diet has been studied in detail, ungulates have been found to predominate, though the precise species vary according to what is available or most common. Thus Abramov recorded a high frequency of Manchurian wapiti (like red deer) being eaten in the Primorski Krai region of Siberia; Karanth observed a preference for gaur in Nagarahole; and Raghu Chundawat has found slightly more nilgai (blue bull) in the diet in Panna than elsewhere simply because there are more nilgai there than in other study areas.

Recent researches have revealed some fascinating differences in the species, sizes and numbers of prey killed in different parts of the tiger's range. For example, in Siberia the cold weather means that meat does not decay quickly and a tiger can linger for a week or more over a large dinner. In Nagarahole, where the tigers prefer to kill larger prey, they may only have time to eat one-fifth of the available meat. Meanwhile, in Panna, males have been found to include far more domestic cattle in their diet than females do. These observations all have significant conservation implications, so we will investigate them in the penultimate chapter. What is broadly similar everywhere, however, is a tiger's average meat requirement. As a result of his detailed studies of tiger diet in Nagarahole, Karanth has estimated that a male tiger needs 3600 kg (7920 lb) of living meat to sustain him for a year. A female, being considerably smaller, needs about 3000 kg (6600 lb). By his reckoning, since the average weight of a chital doe is 50 kg (110 lb), a tiger will need to kill 72 does a year, or one every five days, while a tigress without cubs may get by on 60. Chital is the 'typical' prey species. Tigers kill them wherever they occur, although where larger prey is reasonably plentiful tigers prefer it, as Karanth has shown – and it is easy to see why. If a tiger can kill prey weighing 100 kg (220 lb) it will, in theory, only have to exert itself 36 times a year.

But tigers don't lead theoretical lives. In reality they eat as often as possible and they kill when they get the chance, even if they are not particularly hungry. Valmik Thapar describes an incident that he witnessed in 1985 when the Ranthambhore tigress Noon had been fast asleep for several hours in a clump of grass. She was woken by the rustling of a careless langur walking towards her and instantly, with a bound and a pounce, she caught and killed it. A male langur only weighs about 15 kg (33 lb), which is a modest meal for a tiger since that includes skin and bones. Mel Sunquist, working in Chitwan, calculated that an average tiger ate 15–18 kg (33–40 lb) of meat from a kill in a single night's feeding. In Kanha, Schaller recorded two tigresses together eating more than 40 kg (88 lb) from a cow at one sitting and a male eating 79 kg (174 lb) of a barasingha over three nights – roughly 26 kg (57 lb) per meal. From his numerous observations at kills he concluded that an adult tiger could easily work its way through 18–27 kg (40–60 lb) a night, probably much more, which Charles McDougal confirms in his book *The Face of the Tiger*, mentioning a male tiger eating 35 kg (77 lb) of meat in one go.

In fact, a tiger will sometimes eat itself to a standstill – or rather a lie-still. In November 2001 my friend Vivek Sharma and I had lost track of one of the more reliable dominant males, B2,

Below: Chital (spotted deer) are one of the most important prey species for tigers in India. Tigers need to kill approximately one of them a week.

in Bandhavgarh in Madhya Pradesh. He had not been seen for a couple of days, so we thought he might be lying up on a kill and we went in search of him, following our noses. Along one of the quieter tracks we came upon a strong whiff of newly decaying meat. A very new kill hardly smells but on the second or (in cooler weather) third day it acquires a rich, dense, off-meat smell – not the same as the utterly foul, sweetly sick death-stench that clings to clothes and hair, but not a smell you'd want at your wedding. We were accompanied by a senior forest officer, so Vivek, always enthusiastic, asked permission to investigate. It is never a good idea to blunder around near a tiger's kill and, though he was careful not to plunge blindly into the undergrowth, it was probably just as well that he didn't find anything. Back in the jeep and driving a little further up the track, we glimpsed a tiny patch of something white showing against the tawny dust down in the dry river bed, or *nallah*, that ran parallel with us. It was only about 20 m (65 feet) away, but it was almost totally obscured by the dip of the bed and the undergrowth in front. Through my binoculars I could see that it was slowly moving up and down and, by standing on top of the jeep, I could make out part of the white, swollen belly of a very fat tiger sleeping almost on its back. We summoned the elephants and waited for them to trudge the half-hour journey to us while the tiger lay like a big striped

bellows. When the first elephant arrived, we mounted and pushed our way into the *nallah* to photograph him. It was B2 and he had eaten so much that his stomach looked like a second tiger. There must have been most of something else inside and he either couldn't move or really didn't want to. As the morning wore on other excited tourists arrived and were shuttled back and forth to look at him but he never budged, preferring to lie there among the clicking cameras than pull himself to his feet. I still wonder what would have happened if Vivek had walked in upon him.

A tiger's favourite cut of meat seems to be rump steak. Even though tigers often kill by biting with a stranglehold round the neck, and then drag the kill by the head to safe cover, they usually start feeding from the other end, eating the haunches first. After a full feed they need to drink, so as soon as they can move comfortably they pad off to the nearest water hole, pulling the kill under a bush or under a canopy of long grass to hide it if they have to travel far. If a tiger is undisturbed and doesn't stumble on other prey in the meantime, it will return to its meal until almost everything has been eaten. The largest bones of big animals may get gnawed but not devoured, and the vegetable contents of the stomach are left, but intestines are often eaten; Schaller listed the only remnants of a three-month-old chital fawn as being 'a piece of cranium, three pieces of long bone, one metatarsus, and four bone splinters'.

After the kill

A tiger's kill is an important event in the forest. In the first place, of course, the victim leaves a gap in its own community. The death of a prime male sambar, for instance, may see his favourite patch invaded by younger males looking to improve their access to the hinds, and this could have a temporary impact on local vegetation. The loss of a chital fawn means, for the other deer, the squandering of a seven-month gestation period and all the food used to sustain the pregnant female. But in a wider scientific sense, a kill means the redistribution of nutrients and there is quite a throng ready to gatecrash the banquet. At the top of the list are more or less invited guests. Tigers often share their meals with other tigers – a mother with her cubs, siblings with each other, and sometimes more distant relatives join the table. As many as nine tigers have been recorded at a single kill and these gatherings – rare as they may be – are so interesting that they merit separate treatment as part of our investigation of the tiger's social life. Sometimes the other tiger is uninvited.

Dominant tigers will push younger ones off their own kills, and big males, who can be 70 per cent bigger than their mates, sometimes displace females. On several occasions Valmik Thapar watched Noon, the tigress that learnt Genghis's hunting tricks round Ranthambhore's lakes, lose her kills to her watching mate, Kublai. No wonder a tiger tucks into the choicest part of its kill as soon as it has secured it.

While tigers will steal from leopards and even crocodiles, it is very rare for other species to steal a kill directly from them. The only possible candidate is the Indian wild dog. This dog, weighing about 20 kg (44 lb), is a beautiful deep-red colour, with black tail and dark face, and because it hunts in family groups it is a formidable killer. Dogs are rare and conflicts with tigers infinitely rare, but there have been records of dogs killing tigers and the

Opposite: B2 with a very full stomach (see text p. 32).
Below: Wild dog (or dhole) is one of the few animals that, in a large group, can chase a tiger off a kill.

cause seems sometimes to have been a dispute over dinner. Schaller quotes a fascinating account by Kenneth Anderson (1954) in which a tigress is exhausted in a fight with an 'advance party' of half a dozen dogs, kills one and escapes. She is then pursued by the rest of the pack – a further 23 – and is finally cornered, killed and eaten 8 km (5 miles) away, at the cost of five more dead dogs.

Most scavengers, however, will only press their claims when the tiger is absent. These include jackal, the rare striped hyena, civet cat, mongoose, jungle cat, leopard cat (an animal I have never seen), wild boar and crocodile. Leopards will eat carrion but live in mortal fear of tigers, and some writers claim to have found sloth bears at tiger kills. Probably all these mammals, and others, will help themselves to a tiger's meat if they can but Schaller's studies put scavenging into perspective. His analysis of the jackal's diet in Kanha, for instance, showed that they were eating 80 per cent small rodents and that remains of ungulates of any sort – including domestic goats – were found in fewer than 4 per cent of faeces.

From a tiger's point of view, the most irritating scavengers are probably birds. Colourful tree-pies and red-billed blue magpies will visit kills but the most persistent birds are crows. The small, pure-black jungle crow is usually the first creature to spot a kill. Their harsh cawing as they gather in the trees above is a sure give-away and their compact size means that they can worm their way under the forest cover to where the tiger has hidden its meal. Crows are rarely absent from a kill but they mostly clean up the discarded bits. India, however, has eight species of vulture, four of which – the largest species, lammergeier, the Eurasian and Himalayan griffons and the cinereous or black vulture – are more or less confined to the northern high mountains. The other four species – the black-and-white Egyptian vulture, the white-rumped vulture, the long-billed vulture with its dark neck, and the red-headed or king vulture – are widespread throughout peninsular India where most tigers are found and, being smaller, are more amenable to forest life. Vultures can make heavy inroads on the meaty parts of a tiger's kill but they need sufficient space to manoeuvre. Although they use the forest trees as roosts and lookout points and will flap up and down from them, vultures are more attracted to kills where there is an open patch nearby for ease of take-off and landing. Kills in grassland and stony ravines are particularly prone to visits from vultures, and tigers know this, scratching earth and leaves over meat they are leaving behind. If a tiger finds vultures present when he returns to a carcass, he will charge them and, if any are too slow or too fat to rise, he will batter them out of the air and kill them. But tigers probably earn as much from vultures as they lose to them. Tigers will eat meat they haven't killed and may well be guided to carrion by the sight of vultures on the move. The carcasses of animals that die of old age, disease, starvation and fights with each other belong to everyone. They are quickly cleaned up by the scavenging brigade and tigers are not above joining in. A BBC film-team in Kaziranga watched a tiger arrive at the remains of a dead elephant. It grabbed a large piece of the elephant's trunk and ran off, holding it aloft like a giant sausage.

Finally, when a tiger makes a kill, the universal dinner gong that brings the crow, jackal or vulture is also heard in the soil. Here the invertebrate reprocessing community of ants, beetles, worms and bacterial microbes completes the cleaning job. They render the scraps of discarded skin and bone into usable elements – such as calcium and phosphorus – that will subsequently be taken up once more by plants and recycled again from plant to herbivore to carnivore. In most of the tiger's range hot weather ensures that the process of decay – the passing of a kill from stench to dust – is very quick. The tiger has only a few days to bolt down its meal before the remains rejoin the ecosystem. Where this does not happen, in the cold-climate regions of Siberia for instance, it has an impact on tiger behaviour, enabling them to survive in areas where prey exists at much lower densities.

Opposite: Tigers don't like vultures taking their prey.
Below: Large-billed or jungle crows are rarely absent from
a kill and sometimes wild boar will scavenge a carcass.

Do animals have individual preferences?

Who initiates courtship?

At what age do tigers first mate?

How do tigers find a mate?

How long does mating last?

Do tigresses mate with more than one male
at a time?

Does the season influence mating activity?

Courtship and Mating
Pairing Up Well

In April 1997 I sat with Deb Roy watching a herd of elephants in Assam. We were sitting on the steep banks of a long ox-bow lake in Kaziranga National Park. Most days the elephants would emerge from the distant forest and cross the meadows to the lake, where they would drink before swimming over to the dense beds of elephant grass on our side. On this particular morning we had counted 19 elephants, halfway over the meadows, when we noticed a second group of six about 2 km (1¼ miles) away. Both parties consisted entirely of females and calves.

Teenage males start bothering the females, so between the ages of 13 and 15 they are usually edged out of the herd to join a bachelor gang where they learn to grow up. As the two groups converged to within 1 km (½ mile) of each other, the apparent leader of the smaller party detached herself and walked purposefully on her own towards the main herd; 19 elephants quietly watched her approach and, when she was 100 m (320 feet) away, a senior female walked out to meet her. They stood calmly head to head, touching trunks and cheeks, and then an extraordinary thing happened. One of the other elephants suddenly broke ranks. She raised her trunk, opened her mouth in what can only be described as a huge grin and galloped up to the newcomer. They literally hugged, entwining their trunks in a conspicuously affectionate embrace. These two elephants were clearly very pleased to see each other. The visitor then proceeded to greet every member of the herd, stopping by each one, sometimes stroking them with her trunk, sometimes granting a brief touch or just a nod. Even the smallest calves were acknowledged. What was most interesting was that she had a different style of greeting for each elephant and that she seemed to be much more fond of some than of others. When she had finished and had fed with them for a while, she made her way back to her own group.

Everyone who has studied intelligent social mammals – elephants, baboons, chimps, hyenas even – has found that relationships are based on individual characteristics and preferences. Social success and elevated rank does not depend solely on the exercise of brute strength but on the forging and maintenance of alliances between individuals. I was in Kaziranga to film and study one-horned Indian rhinos. At first glance they

seemed incapable of social graces, being solitary and bad-tempered. They seemed only to have three positions: head down to feed – the most usual; head up to sniff or snort at anything that approached; head down to charge. But over the next two years I realized there might be more to their social life than was thought. Some adults were clearly much more comfortable with one another than others. One female had two nine-month-old calves, which stayed with her throughout my time in the field. Were they twins? Twins seem not to be recorded in Asian rhinos. Or had she adopted an orphan – in which case was it her sister's calf; her mother's; a friend's? I don't believe adoption has been

recorded, either. And what to make of four rhinos, two mothers and two full-grown calves, who walked across the meadows in single file, each with her head on the rump of the rhino in front? Then there were adults that seemed to like to sit beside each other in the wallows, and others that chased everyone out of the way. The simple, obvious truth was that no rhino was exactly the same in temperament as another.

On the scale of sociability, tigers lie somewhere between elephants and rhinos – perhaps closer to rhinos. But the point is that tigers (like all animals) are individuals, not automatons. If we admit the possibility that tigers (like elephants and even rhinos) feel and express personal preferences, then nowhere is this likely to be more significant than in the business of courtship, mating and the rearing of cubs. Radio-collars, camera traps and long-term field work enable us to study tigers as

Opposite: Elephants form intense attachments and their personal relationships are the basis for herd dynamics.
Below: One-horned rhino are mostly solitary.

individuals and the more we do, the more we realize that there is a wide range of different behaviour, all of it 'normal'. It is normal, for example, for male tigers to kill young cubs, to ignore young cubs, to play with young cubs or even perhaps to help rear them. As we shall see, what an individual male actually does will depend on his temperament, his circumstances and the specific relationships he has with the other tigers in his area.

Courtship etiquette

Before exploring all these fascinating variables, however, let us start where tigers start: with the process of courtship. Courtship is initiated by the female. This is true among most animals – as it is among human beings, though we don't always admit that. The reason it is true is that the aim of courtship is reproduction and, since the chances of reproductive success are reduced if the female is unreceptive, sensible males reserve their precious

energy until their services are welcome. I saw this amply demonstrated by red deer in Ireland when I was filming them there in the mid-1990s. Old-fashioned naturalists used to describe the red deer stag as the monarch of the glen, who beat up all competitors and was rewarded by the right to rule a harem of docile females who would cater to his every whim. This is misleading. One October day in the Wicklow Mountains I watched a stag roaring out his dominance before selecting a likely-looking hind for his delectation. She walked seductively ahead of him and raised her tail, inviting him to sniff and 'flehmen' (see p. 79) but just as he jumped up to mount her she slipped forward a couple of paces and he missed. They walked another 50 m (160 feet) together and again she raised her tail and he sniffed and jumped and missed again. On and on they went through the tall heather, with her tantalizing him and staying just out of reach. It was an unseasonably hot day. He was a huge animal with a fine head of antlers but, as the sun rose higher and she led him further into the shimmering distance, he began to tire and drag his feet. She didn't stop for a couple of kilometres and by the time he was permitted to mount her, he was in no state to rule anyone.

A male tiger has more than mere exhaustion to fear from an unreceptive tigress. Even though he may weigh at least half as much again as she does, she is still the second most dangerous animal in the jungle after him and it pays to treat her with respect. Indeed, courtship among most predators can be fraught with tension. In birds of prey, for instance, this is accentuated by the fact that females, because they have to be able to hunt while burdened by developing eggs, are bigger than males. In sparrowhawks and peregrines the size difference can be nearly double, so the males approach the nest with noisy calls to remind

Left: Radio-collars allow us to identify and follow individual tigers.
Opposite: Scent-marking is an important way for tigers to communicate when looking for a mate.

their beloved that they are bringing food, rather than that they are food themselves! A tiger does not have this problem but still he prefers to avoid injury and will not usually push his luck with an unfriendly tigress.

Tigers potentially become sexually mature at about two and a half years. In practice, however, they are unlikely to become sexually active until they have established themselves as residents within a home range where they feel confident. For females this usually means around three to three and a half years, for males a year or so later. When a tigress comes into season the fluctuations in her hormones cause a change in her behaviour. She becomes restless and begins to pace her home range. She leaves more scent marks than usual, rubs her cheeks and flanks against bushes and trees, smells and flehmens at her own urine and rolls on the ground. She also tends to become more vocal, moaning and 'sneezing' – a blowing action through the nose sometimes called 'prustening'. When she is really serious she roars. A roaring tigress can be heard over several kilometres and may attract more than one male, though that may not be her intention. Tigresses, again like most females, are quite particular as to whom they mate with. The first attempt with a new male is often unsuccessful. Perhaps the tigers are too nervous with each other, afraid of getting hurt or simply uncomfortable. In any case, it seems that the better they know each other and the longer they have been resident within their respective ranges, the more likely the female is to conceive. The breeding success of a very stable, long-term male resident in Chitwan, Tiger 105, with 51 cubs to his name (see p. 86), is a good example. Furthermore, a tigress's own physiology protects her from injudicious coupling for she requires the stimulus of frequent bouts of mating over several days before she is likely to complete her ovulation. A quick fumble in the dark will not do the trick. This means that even if her roars attract several males and a cheeky youngster reaches her first, she is unlikely to get saddled with the 'inferior' offspring of an unprotective transient.

Mating

A full mating session is a prodigious performance. Ideally the tigress will have attracted the resident male in her area with whom she is already familiar. They then find a secluded spot, often in dense bushes or long grass, where they can hole up together undisturbed for a few days. They spend a lot of time lying down about 5 m (16 feet) apart. If the male approaches before she is ready, trying to force the issue, the tigress can be very aggressive. It may be that tigers and tigresses that don't know each other well misread the signals but there is no doubt that some matings are less friendly than others. A sensible male watches the female carefully for signs of enthusiasm. When she is ready, she usually stands up, walks a few paces towards him, crouches down in a sphinx-like position called 'lordosis' and turns her tail to the side. The male stands as soon as she does and mounts her when she crouches, usually holding the scruff of her neck in his teeth. The love-making appears quite perfunctory, rarely lasting more than 10 or 20 seconds. And the male has to be on the alert because the moment he has finished, his sweetheart is likely to twist round onto her back and swipe at him with a forepaw. A fresh, vigorous male springs backwards with surprising agility and avoids the slap. But as she approaches ovulation her requirements become more and more frequent. He may have to perform every 15 minutes – and woe betide him if he flags.

Sooner or later most males get caught: 50 or 60 orgasms over a couple of days can take it out of a chap and this is what is expected of most male tigers. It is not surprising that the Sanskrit word for tiger is *viagra* and that foolish humans have set such store by the 'medicinal' value of tiger penises. The sight of a tired male tiger sitting alone in the jungle with a bloody scratch

Opposite: During mating the male usually holds the scruff of the female's neck in his teeth.

on his nose, or nursing a punctured paw and looking sorry for himself, is a common signal that a local love affair has passed its climacteric. There are several possible explanations for why a tigress becomes so tetchy. One may be that she is scarcely house-trained. Being a predominantly solitary animal, she may find the invasion of her space degrading and therefore reasserts her need for a bit of distance each time the brief urgings of ecstasy are complete. The swipe may also be a good test of the male's fitness for the job. I have certainly noticed that a tigress tends to become more irritable towards the end of the affair, possibly because ovulation has taken place and many further matings become superfluous, or because the male is annoying her by

being too slow – so perhaps the swipe is a way of finishing. When the tiger finally gets it on the nose he knows it's time to resume his bachelor life.

Unfortunately, I have not been lucky to witness enough wild-tiger couplings to assess the average tigress's motives – I'm not sure anyone has. What I have seen so far, however, is quite similar to lion courtship. Tigers and lions are very close relatives and so, in this respect, one observation about lions may be relevant here. Of the many lion matings I have seen, no two have been identical. Sometimes the lion has been extremely tentative – on one occasion so much so that the lioness got fed up with him and gave him his marching orders. Other times the lion has been

more dominant but has still received his swipe on the nose. But occasionally I have observed what it is tempting to describe as real tenderness between a couple: they have rubbed faces before mating, or the lioness has rolled on her back afterwards, but the cuff has been a caress. Sometimes I have found the two fast asleep wrapped in a lovers' embrace – face to face, their paws round each other's necks. If elephants have a different greeting for every elephant they know, it is not unreasonable to suppose that a lioness or tigress has a different class of swipe for different males. The chances are that some tigers and tigresses get to 'like' each other and are capable of showing a tigerly sort of affection.

In most cases a tigress will mate with the dominant resident male in her neighbourhood. This is natural: his dominance ensures that she acquires strong genes for her cubs and the continuity of his presence will provide protection for them. But it is not the whole story. Recent observations have turned up some curious anomalies. One of Raghu Chundawat's radio-collared females in Panna has apparently been recorded mating with two different big males during the same period. Was she hedging her bets or fooling both tigers into thinking they would have an interest in her cubs? Even more surprising, the respected Indian film-maker Naresh Bedi tells me that in March 2002 he filmed two males taking it in turns to mate with the same female in Kanha (see p. 94).

If the tigress does not become pregnant, she is likely to come back into oestrus again within a few weeks. The oestrus cycles of tigers have been investigated mainly in zoos and found to be quite diverse: 100 cycles recorded in nine captive Bengal tigresses by D. G. Kleiman, in a study published in 1974, varied from 12 to 86 days, with an average of 49.1. A 1987 report by

U. S. Seal, R. L. Tilson and others observed five captive Siberian tigers and noted an average cycle of 25 days. Interestingly, both studies reported a seasonal influence. The Bengal tigresses had 50 per cent more cycles between October and March, compared with April to September. The Siberian tigresses' cycles were confined to the period from late January to early June, and separate analysis of 1239 captive births revealed a peak from April to June. The apparent accentuation of seasonal mating behaviour in Siberian tigresses is not surprising. They live on a line of latitude many degrees further north than Bengal tigers (Sikhote-Alin is at 45° North, whereas, for instance, Kanha is at 22° North), where seasonal climate differences are more pronounced and light is an obvious hormonal trigger. Further south the hours of daylight are roughly even throughout the year and the only seasonal event is the monsoon, which occurs between June and September, peaking in July and August.

Consequently, on the Indian subcontinent mating may occur and cubs may be born in any month of the year. Down south in Nagarahole, Ullas Karanth has recorded a radio-collared tigress mating in January, March, May, July and October, and Charles McDougal found 12 separate litters of cubs in Chitwan in Nepal spread over nine different months. Nevertheless, even in the subcontinent most observers – for example, McDougal in Chitwan, Arjun Singh in Dudhwa and George Schaller in Kanha – have reported an increase in sexual activity in winter and early spring.

The first mating attempt between a new pair of tigers is often unsuccessful. The animals may be nervous and need to learn to trust one another. Maachli – the Ranthambhore tigress followed in the BBC films *The Tigers' Fortress* and *Danger in Tiger Paradise* – is a good example. During the filming period she produced two litters by two different mates (the first mate died) and each conception required at least two bouts of courtship. Actually, the second mating was also extremely interesting for other reasons, but we will look at those later.

Opposite: Tigers that know each other well can sometimes seem genuinely affectionate.

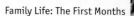

Where do tigresses give birth?

Why is a tigress's pregnancy so short?

How big are cubs at birth?

When do cubs start eating meat?

What is the mortality rate for young cubs?

Why do tigers sometimes kill tiger cubs?

Are orphaned tigers ever adopted?

Might a tigress seduce a strange male
to protect her cubs?

What is the father's role in the life of the cubs?

Family Life
The First Months

When a tigress becomes pregnant her priorities change. Previously her only interests have been to feed herself and, during the brief periods of oestrus, to find a mate. Now she focuses on finding the right place to give birth to her cubs. Her selection criteria are based on safety and a ready supply of food and water. These last two are especially important because her cubs will be very dependent in their early months. It will not be safe for her to leave them for long periods, so she will be confined to just a small area of her range. The most impregnable den is of little use if there are no juicy deer in the vicinity. In any case, in choosing her birthing den a tigress's idea of safety might not be ours.

Tigresses seem to be creatures of habit – even, sometimes, when habit has mistreated them. Fiona and Mel Sunquist tell an interesting story of tigress Number 1 (101), the first tigress to be radio-collared in Chitwan by the Smithsonian team. In the mid-1970s she gave birth to a litter in a dense thicket of grass but sadly this was engulfed in a grass fire and the cubs were burnt alive. She came into season again within 15 days and mated with the same father – the famous Tiger 105 – but it apparently took

four months and several couplings before she conceived again. And what did Number 1 do? She had the new litter in exactly the same patch of elephant grass. This time villagers came to cut the grass and, after several days of bouncing out and roaring at them, she had to give up and move the cubs 1.5 km (1 mile) away. She then ceded much of her range to her daughter, who also mated with 105 (her own father) and birthed her first litter in another den previously used by Number 1.

Probably a key factor in a tigress's notion of safety is invisibility. Most dens are in tangled domes of long grass, like Number 1's, in dense thickets or in caves. The cubs are born on average 103 days after conception. This relatively short gestation

Below and opposite: Tiger cubs spend their first weeks hidden in the birthing den and live almost exclusively on their mother's milk for their first two months.

period – similar to a lion's, a few days longer than a leopard's – is found in most hunting carnivores. Small cats and most of the dogs have an even shorter gestation, usually around 60 days. There are good evolutionary reasons for this. A tigress, like the other predators, has to hunt almost every day, so she cannot be burdened by enormous, highly developed unborn kittens. It is more efficient to get them out of her body quickly, relying on her own prowess to defend them from other predators while they mature outside the womb. For herbivores that are prey species, the opposite applies. A chital in the late stages of pregnancy may be slightly handicapped in a crisis if she has to escape suddenly but her daily feeding is unaffected. It is best for her to produce a precocious, well-developed baby since that calf will have to move with the herd, feed itself and perhaps even run from a tiger within hours of its birth. Consequently, the chital's gestation period is double that of the tiger's.

The disadvantage of this system, from the tiger's point of view, is that the cubs are born blind and helpless. The mortality rate is high and so – unlike herbivores, which invest in one or at most two young – carnivores have multiple births. Tigers can produce as many as seven cubs, Charles McDougal mentioned a tigress in Ranthambhore in 1976–7 that had raised five cubs to the age of nine months and there was a tigress in Bandhavgarh with four well-grown youngsters in 2000–1 and another in

2002–3. The average litter size in India, however, is closer to three (George Schaller quoted 2.8 on the basis of 79 zoo births), and in 1987 V. Spitsin, P. Romanov and others (in *Tigers of the World*) reported an average of two during the previous 19 years in Siberia's Sikhote-Alin Biosphere Reserve.

The cubs' first months

Cubs are tiny at birth, usually weighing 1.2–1.8 kg (2½–4 lb). To give a proportionate idea of how small they are, this is approximately $\frac{1}{150}$ of the size they will reach if they manage to attain adulthood. Compare that to a human baby, whose birth weight is roughly $\frac{1}{15}$ of its adult weight. The baby tigers won't open their eyes for at least a week. Schaller reports a zoo cub waiting 17 days before it looked at the world. Although they acquire their milk teeth after a month, tiger cubs remain concealed in the den for most (if not all) of their second month, still feeding exclusively on milk. Dave Smith monitored the movements of tigresses with young cubs for the Smithsonian Tiger Ecology Project in Chitwan and found that during this critical period a mother was almost always at home, nursing her babies and, even when hunting for herself, she never strayed more than 1.4 km (¾ mile) away from them.

We have little certainty about the precise mortality rates among very young cubs because no one but their mother sees them in these early weeks. This is a period of absolute secrecy. The mother and cubs are quiet and she is active only for brief hunting excursions. Smith told me that on one occasion he had to investigate a birthing den. He crawled down a long, low, rank tunnel of bent elephant grass in a state of barely controlled terror. He knew the mother was close by, might give the radio-receiver the slip and appear behind him in the mouth of the tunnel. His other worry was that his scent around the cubs would disrupt her nursing but in the event both he and the cubs survived. Not surprisingly, observers do not make a habit of poking their noses into tiger dens, most of which go undetected or at least unapproached.

The first glimpse most of us will get of very young cubs – and then only if we are very lucky – is when they begin to taste their first meat and the tigress moves them away from the birth den to hunt in other parts of her range. The precise moment when cubs begin to wash down a few solids with their milk varies from family to family and from place to place. Captive Siberian tigers have been recorded coming quite late to meat, at around ten weeks, whereas Bengal tiger cubs usually start eating solids at six to eight weeks. Because life in the wild birthing den is so private, so rarely observed, there is still some controversy as to whether tigresses ever regurgitate meat for their partially weaned cubs. Some authorities (McDougal, for instance) rule this out but regurgitation has been observed among big cats in captivity, so perhaps it does happen occasionally if a kill is too far from the den. On the whole, however, when the cubs are ready for meat they leave the den to eat it off the bone.

Opposite: If they are disturbed, the female will carry her cubs to a new den.

Above: Small cubs are under orders to stay where they are put.

From this moment of a cub's first public appearance until the end of its first year of life there is a one in three chance that it will die. In Siberia, according to Spitsin and Romanov, of 35 cubs born between 1966 and 1982, 15 died in their first year – a mortality rate of 43 per cent. Studies of captive tigers have shown that stomach disorders caused by *E. coli* infection are a common cause of death in cubs. But even healthy wild tiger cubs inhabit a dangerous world. Accidents, fires and floods take a toll; so do other predators. There are no detailed studies on the frequency of predation on tiger cubs but until they are five or six months old they are vulnerable, especially in a place like Kanha that they share with wolves, wild dogs and leopards. Although the tigress is attentive, once the cubs are eating meat she has to conceal them for long periods while she hunts. There must be a critical period at around four months, when they are eating a lot and so she must leave them more often, but they are still quite inept at self-defence.

Infanticide

During these early months there is one predator cubs fear more than all the rest put together: a male tiger that is not their father. Infanticide among big cats is a fact of life – as it is among domestic cats. It is not common but it is 'normal'. Why would a tiger kill baby tigers? The answer is that it is a classic example of the interests of the gene taking precedence over those of the species. For tigers in general it is a bad thing that males kill cubs but for the individual tiger and the particular genes he carries it can be vital. Understanding why helps us to appreciate that natural selection and survival of the fittest are not quite the clockwork processes we may have thought.

Male tigers may not become breeding residents until their fifth or sixth year, sometimes even later. From that point on, the window of opportunity for the individual male to breed is surprisingly small. According to the Smithsonian Project, the average male only survives as a breeder for 33 months. Of course, there are exceptions. The Smithsonian's Tiger 105 lasted six years; Bahadur Bhale, the subject of my *Man-Eater: To Be or Not To Be* film, had a four-and-a-half year rule; and Charger, the famous male of Bandhavgarh, lived until he was 17 and is thought to have fathered his last litter a year before he died. But for every one of these success stories there are numerous less fortunate males. They lack the family support system that females enjoy by settling

close to one another (see p. 83), and there are fewer home ranges available to them and more competition for those that become free. Consequently, more males are killed or injured in fights and are poached or poisoned or disabled by hunting injuries. So for most males time is short and the urge to sow their particular seeds is acute. If, after settling a home range, they find that the females in their area all have cubs, they have a problem. Rearing cubs normally suppresses the onset of oestrus in a mother tiger. Once her cubs have been conceived, she is unlikely to come back into season until they are independent. A young tiger cannot effectively hunt for itself until its adult canines have developed and that does not happen until it is around 16 months old; then it has to learn to use them. The earliest a tigress is likely to mate again is when her cubs are 18 months old – and in practice they often stay with her until they are two or even two and a half years old.

If the newly settled male waits good-naturedly until the cubs are grown, then he may get no chance (or at best one chance) to sire cubs later on the mother. If, however, a tragic accident should befall the little babies, the mother will come into oestrus again within weeks, maybe even days. Mating with the newly bereaved mother will mean that the next litter is definitely the new male's and within two years he will even get a second opportunity to establish his own genes. This is what 'my' tiger, Bahadur Bhale (Bhale just means 'male'), the subject of my *Man-Eater* film, appears to have done. According to Dave Smith's notes, Bahadur Bhale was a young tiger in December 1983, hanging around female 122, who had very small cubs by the resident male, Bangi Bhale. Those cubs disappeared and three

months later, in March 1984, probably just when 122 came back into oestrus, Smith actually witnessed a spectacular fight between the two males, which Bahadur Bhale seems to have won. At any rate he remained in the range and mated with 122 while the old male, Bangi Bhale, departed. Subsequently Bangi Bhale met an unhappy fate, which is described in *Man on the Menu* (see p. 107).

Infanticide has been studied in greater detail in lions. In his ground-breaking study of lions in the Serengeti, popularized in *Golden Shadows, Flying Hooves*, George Schaller calculated that pride males had an even shorter period of tenure than male tigers – less than two years. Consequently, infanticide was a common outcome of the 'take-over' of a pride of lionesses by new males. He describes one particularly grisly battle which resulted in the death of one pride male and – by an unknown hand – of three young cubs. Two of these corpses were carried off by invading males but what happened next is an eloquent reminder that however much science we bring to bear on its behaviour, we may never fully fathom how a big cat thinks:

> One of the cubs was left at the kill site. I waited by it all day to see how lioness D would respond when she found her dead offspring. I did not know what to expect – indifference or sentiment. She came just as the last light failed. After sniffing the carcass and licking it briefly, she ate it. Fifteen minutes later only the head and forepaws remained, and as I sat there in the dark listening to her crunch the bones, I realized that I still had not penetrated the mystery of the lion's brain.

Some tigers appear to be more bloodthirsty than others. When I was filming in Bardia in western Nepal in 1992, the park trackers said that one of the males – which we unimaginatively dubbed Jack-the-Ripper – had killed two adult females. Certainly,

Previous page: Broken Tail (see text on p. 69) aged nine months old in Ranthambhore.
Opposite: Even after three months cubs are vulnerable and the female moves them with her around her range.

tigresses occasionally take a terrible beating in defence of their cubs. In April 1999 the BBC screened a Wildlife Special called *Tiger*, one of the best tiger films ever made. It was shot in Kanha, much of it by the young American cameraman Chip Houseman, who was tragically killed in an aeroplane crash in Thailand just before the film was completed. Chip kept a diary recording what happened to the 'heroine' of the film, Lakshmi. She was rearing three cubs – two males and a female – and had to defend them in four serious fights during the two years of filming. The problem was an extremely aggressive male. On 11 July 1997 Lakshmi was badly injured by him, though her cubs were saved and the elephant drivers found the male eating someone else's one-month-old cub. Then in January 1998 he had another go at her, wounding her so severely that she probably never recovered. By 31 January she was barely able to move and although there were rumours that she survived, Chip never saw her again. By that time her cubs were 13 months old – a bit big for infanticide. A cub of that size, especially one defended by mother and siblings, can damage a male even though it is no match for him. At this point the risk of incurring an injury begins to outweigh for the male the advantage of bringing the female back into oestrus. After all, by now he has only a few more months to wait and she may be his without a squabble. Consequently, almost all cases of true infanticide – the wiping out of a litter to stimulate oestrus – involve much younger cubs, of nine months or less.

The role of kinship in tiger society

The subsequent fate of Lakshmi's cubs was interesting. If Lakshmi died, then her cubs, at 13 or even 14 months, would have been too young to hunt for themselves. They may, however, have learnt to scavenge the kills of other tigers. Lakshmi's range was taken over by two of her daughters from previous litters. One of these, now eight years old, had two enormous two-year-old male cubs,

and in March 1998 the film-crew saw the little orphaned female, which they had named Sundari, approach the family. Hugh Miles, who produced the film with Mike Birkhead, described what happened next in a *BBC Wildlife Magazine* article in April 1999:

> The female snarled at her with considerable aggression. But the big males largely ignored her, and she even had the temerity to walk up and sniff the rear end of one of them without any hostile response.
>
> Within days, Sundari had charmed her way into being accepted by her half-sister – a most unusual turn of events. She was even allowed to curl up and sleep with them and share their kills.

According to the magazine article, Lakshmi's two orphaned male cubs also made it to independence, though this is perhaps more doubtful. Whatever their ultimate fate, Sundari did survive. I saw her in January 2003. She walked past my elephant, hissed at me and then scent-marked the ground and two bushes on her way to meet the cubs of her second litter. I saw all three of them together in April 2003. The fact that Sundari was successfully adopted by her much older half-sister is a graphic illustration of the importance of kinship in tiger society. In fact, no tiger is an island. Tigers are not just a bunch of aggressive solitary individuals wandering the jungle beating each other up. There is growing evidence that they recognize their own relatives and are more tolerant towards them than they are to strangers. Sundari's story shows that the network of relationships in an area can be supportive, though it is females that are most likely to benefit from the tolerance of kin because, as we shall see, the pattern of

Opposite: After the death of her mother, Sundari seems to have been 'adopted' by her half-sister (see text p. 56). She is now an adult with her second litter of cubs.

settlement means that tigresses usually end up being related to their neighbours.

There are indications, however, that kinship also influences the behaviour of males. Lakshmi's misfortunes prove that a male tiger can pose a lethal threat to cubs of all ages. One obvious flashpoint is at a kill. Even a kill made by a female for her cubs may be appropriated by an aggressive male and this can erupt into conflict. But the mere existence of a female who is otherwise engaged can be a provocation to a male, so tigresses try to keep their cubs (especially their young cubs) under wraps. In Kanha, in November 2001, females with cubs stopped using the superb hunting grounds in the open Mukki meadows because a new big male had taken up residence there and they did not want to risk a meeting with him.

Violent and aggressive males seem to be more common in Kanha than in other well-observed reserves like Ranthambhore and Bandhavgarh. If so, the explanation may lie in degrees of kinship. Kanha is a large reserve – nearly 3000 sq km (1160 square miles), including buffer zones and nearby forests – and it is part of a mosaic of great reserves and forests that are scattered over southern Madhya Pradesh. This is a region where a male tiger can disperse properly. In theory he can travel hundreds of kilometres and settle far away from his natal range, where he may not be related to any of the new tigers he meets. Unconstrained by genetic, familial promptings, he might demand mating rights with absolute aggression – and another tiger's cubs may be fair game. Ranthambhore, on the other hand, covers only about 400 sq km (155 square miles) and the forest area is isolated

in a dry desert of populous farmland. The opportunities to disperse are much reduced, so related males are probably forced to settle close to each other and to their own sisters, aunts and cousins. Here a new resident male may be aware that his predecessor's cubs are his own half-siblings and so he will be genetically less predisposed to slaughter them in the pursuit of his own chance to mate.

However, this is mere speculation. We don't actually know for certain what the degrees of kinship are among the tigers of Kanha or Ranthambhore or Bandhavgarh because no one has ever tagged a single tiger in any of these reserves. Some brilliant observations and deductions have been made about tigers, especially in Ranthambhore, but the only way to separate individuals beyond doubt, 100 per cent of the time, and study their relationships with other known individuals, is to tag them and follow them on a long-term basis.

Nevertheless, the information that has been gathered so far suggests that male tigers may be less aggressive towards their own relatives and less likely to kill their cubs. Not that a mother tigress will necessarily presume on the goodwill of a cousin or uncle who moves in to replace the father of her cubs. It would seem that she is capable of Machiavellian strategies to keep a new male on side. This was illustrated by a remarkable incident that occurred in Ranthambhore and was recorded in the 2002 BBC film *Danger in Tiger Paradise*. The subject of the film, a tigress called Maachli, had mated with Bombooram, the dominant male of her range, who had himself become famous when he bestowed an audience on President Clinton when he visited the park in 1997. But just when her cubs were born, Bombooram disappeared. There were at least three other males known to be in the vicinity. There was Nick, at two and a half years a bit young to step into Bombooram's shoes. The Chirroli male was a mature tiger, eight or nine years old, but he stayed out on the park perimeter. Finally, there was Chips, at four and a half just reaching his peak and a tiger that was familiar with Maachli's range. As the weeks turned to months, and Bombooram's scent marks faded and his big, broad pugmarks filled with sand, the film-crew expected one of the males to make a bid for Maachli. The likeliest candidate was Chips – and then Maachli's fatherless cubs might be in mortal danger.

In the event it was young Nick who made a play for her. He began to hang around her range and they had a fight, which was filmed. It was an unequal combat because he kept his claws sheathed, whereas she did not, and he ended up with a split paw. Perhaps because he was a younger tiger he was less forceful or confident and Maachli was able to string him along. In any case, nothing else happened until the two cubs, both males, were about 14 months old. This is a critical age, just before the adult canines appear (after which, if necessary, a cub might hunt and kill for itself). At this point Maachli seems to have had a change of heart. One day she was filmed as she set off to seek Nick out herself. She found him on the edge of her range and was seen to lure him into the bushes for a quick fling. This was not a full mating session but a bit on the side. She was not in oestrus; that did not occur for another two and a half months and then she mated in earnest with Nick and subsequently bore his cubs. So what was she doing?

The probable answer is that she was buying time for her cubs so that they could grow up during those crucial extra months with Nick as a protector, or at least not hostile. By granting him some conjugal rights, Maachli was giving him an interest in waiting the few more weeks until she would be truly ready for him. While he waited he would be her first wall of defence against any of the other males in the area. She perhaps chose him, instead of them, either because he was the nearest and most frequent visitor or because his youth and inexperience made him more amenable to manipulation – or even because she liked him. It is also probable that Nick was Maachli's cousin and that kinship may have inclined him to favour her cubs.

This sort of deliberate seductive activity outside oestrus is an area of tiger behaviour about which we know very little and we should be cautious as to how we interpret it. Raghu Chundawat, however, has witnessed something similar in Panna. Where a female has young cubs by a deceased or defeated dominant male, the act of mating with his replacement may be a means of confusing the new male as to the actual paternity of the cubs. She is not in oestrus and she won't get pregnant but he may come to associate the cubs with her and the bond that mating will have forged with her. This might explain why infanticide is not, in fact, more common than it is. It would also be interesting to know whether seduction is more likely to occur, or be successful in preserving the cubs, when the previous male has died rather than been pushed out.

The male as father

Apart from aggressive tendencies, very little is known about the relationship of males to cubs. Because the role of the father in tiger society is not obvious, it has until very recently hardly been studied. Tigers do not live in nuclear families consisting of father, mother and 2.8 cubs. Most males aspire to have more than one family at a time and are at best semi-detached in their relationship to each. On the other hand, they are clearly not indifferent to their offspring. In Ranthambhore, Valmik Thapar noted that males were tolerant of cubs, occasionally sharing water holes and accepting affectionate greetings. The recent presence of a film-team spending several hundred days continuously in the field with the tigers has shed more light on this. Cameraman Colin Stafford Johnson has discovered that it is not unusual to find the males spending time with their cubs and believes that some of them make regular visits to their families, probably to check on them. He has also seen a tigress leave the male in charge of the cubs while she briefly absented herself.

Males will certainly tolerate their own cubs at a kill and on rare occasions may even deliberately share it. Because so much early study of tigers – when tigers were common – was directed at hunting them, this subtle aspect of their lives was hardly noticed. But every single observer in the post-hunting era of the last 40 years who has had long enough in the field to observe males with their cubs has been surprised to discover that they are not without affection. George Schaller gave us the first intimations of this in the 1960s in his observations of a family of three cubs plus adult male and females at a kill

The male rises at 2250 hours and walks to the kill. Two cubs nuzzle his face and neck. He circles the kill, grunting repeatedly, a sound similar to the one emitted by females when inducing small cubs to follow. One cub trails behind the male. He lies down 30 feet [9 m] from the kill, and a cub rubs its body against his.

Raghu Chundawat has taken a particular interest in male tigers and, though his work has far to go, early indications are that the male's role has been underestimated. Males move around more than females. Why? Partly it would seem to get round their ranges checking on their various families. It is also certain that a successful male, holding the same range for several years, provides the same sort of stability that a 'good husband' was thought to provide in traditional human societies. He keeps other males away from the cubs and frees the female to raise them without harassment.

The deepest daily bond, however, is between the cubs and the tigress. They comprise the core family unit and, from everything we know, it would appear that the cubs are the tigress's overriding priority until they attain independence. It is she who actively protects them, stays close to them, nurses them, hunts for them and leads them on to develop hunting skills of their own.

What sounds do the tiger family make?

How do cubs learn to hunt?

What games do tiger cubs play?

How strong are the bonds between siblings?

When do tiger cubs leave home?

How do young tigers survive on their own?

Family Life

Growing Up

Young cubs leave the birthing den with their mother when they are about two months old. From now on she will conceal them in temporary hide-outs, bushes and grass tussocks while she hunts and will usually lead them to food when she has killed. The tigress has a limited but significant vocabulary with which to communicate with her cubs. The most important is the short, sharp grunt, often in threes – ur,ur,ur – which seems to be a sign for the cubs to follow her. Although this is most frequently used with small cubs, I have heard a tigress in Bandhavgarh call her well-grown youngsters away like this, when she was fed up with the attentions of tourist elephants. The friendly sneeze, or prusten, appears to be an affectionate note of greeting, which can also be used between adults, while the woof might be heard if a cub jumps on its mother a bit too suddenly.

Tigers do occasionally purr, though you have to get very close to hear this: a contented tigress being nuzzled by her cubs will sometimes purr. And cubs on their own, especially if they are unhappy, will miaow – a sound otherwise associated with courting couples. Finally, as the cubs grow older and their play becomes increasingly robust, they sometimes snarl and whicker at each other. But a tiger playground is not a noisy place and you may watch tigers for hours without ever hearing a sound.

There are three other calls that the cubs must learn in due course. Roaring is the most obvious. Although most roars involve adults talking to each other – usually about the desire to mate or just to say 'Here I am' – tigers will also roar out of sheer irritation. I have heard a tiger roar when it has missed a kill and Valmik Thapar describes a roar that silenced the querulous alarm calls of deer in Ranthambhore. Roaring, however, is a long-distance communication and so is probably not meant for cubs. The moan, though, is a sort of low-volume, subdued roar and a tiger cub might receive this as a warning if it approaches a kill uninvited. The last call in the tiger's repertoire is described as 'pooking'. By some strange coincidence it is similar to the reverberant alarm call of the sambar – a cross between a hoot and a deep bark – and it too appears to be a warning call. I have only heard it a couple of times and, since it can be difficult to locate and interpret calls in the jungle, I was unable to attribute any meaning to the sound. But George Schaller recorded it three times during his Kanha study and each time it was associated with behaviour near a kill. Perhaps it is not surprising that so much of the tiger's minimal conversation is about food.

Learning by example

There is a popular perception that young animals are actively 'taught' the skills they need to survive by their parents. The idea of the wilderness schoolroom, with tiger cubs lining up for instruction from their wise mother, may be attractive but it does not happen. The nearest most animals come to active parenting is to issue warning alarm calls. Although they may not teach them, however, parents do lead their offspring, probably deliberately, into new situations in which they will learn for themselves. When I have been filming peregrine falcons, for instance, I have noticed that the adults bring food to the nest less frequently as the chicks get close to fledging. This seems to stimulate the wing-flapping and jumping into the air that will eventually blossom into that first magical flight. Similarly, a tigress does not 'teach' her cubs

to hunt but as they grow older she lets them accompany her. Several observers have recorded instances where tigresses have disabled a relatively harmless prey and left the cubs to attempt to finish it off. This has often involved livestock such as goats and bullocks that used to be tethered as live bait and it may be that this unnatural situation allowed mothers and cubs to practise in a way that is rarer in truly wild conditions. Schaller staked out a few young buffaloes in Kanha in the 1960s and recorded a cub biting one in the abdominal wall before the tigress stepped in to dispatch it. On another occasion the tigress threw the buffalo but made no attempt to kill it, leaving it to the 12-month-old cubs to

Opposite: Growing cubs learn important skills by watching their mother.

Below: Cubs practise waiting in ambush for each other.

batter it; ' ...but,' he wrote, 'they failed to kill efficiently, largely confining their attack to biting and clawing around the rump, back and belly, rather than grasping the throat.' At this age a cub, which may weigh 50 kg (110 lb) or more, cannot kill prey its own weight. It has the strength to pull down a deer or a young buffalo but its temporary canines will not puncture the tough skin of the throat and neck. This is the job of the permanent teeth, which may not appear for another three or four months. When they do, the cub has still to discover how the true killing bite works. It may observe its mother delivering this bite but it can

only learn to do it by trial and error – and until those big canines arrive, all efforts will be in vain.

Tiger cubs probably learn most from each other. They do not sit demurely for hours in the bushes. Instead they entertain themselves in bursts of energetic play. They stalk each other, bouncing out on one another to deliver cuffs and surprise buffets, rolling in locked embraces, thrashing out with all four claws. They creep after peacocks and even small birds like bushlarks. They climb trees – a 'useless' lesson, since once they reach adulthood they will find most trees are out of bounds. My friend Vivek Sharma did find a tiger partway up a tree in Bandhavgarh; up in the topmost boughs was the reason for the mountaineering effort: a very uncomfortable leopard. But the tiger's weight was too heavy for its claws and leg muscles and it had to slip backwards down the trunk. Cubs also play with toys. In Bandhavgarh in 2000 there was

Previous page: As they grow up tiger cubs' mock fights become increasingly boisterous.
Below: Adolescent cubs will play in trees – a game they will be too heavy for when they grow up.
Opposite: Mohini's cub and her 'toy' log (see text p. 67).

an adorable young female who adopted a log. Every time I saw her, over several days in November, she would have her little log with her. She carried it between her lips like a cheroot when she was on the move or she would lie on her back with it sticking straight up out of her mouth so that she could swat it from side to side with her forepaws. Tragically, she was killed six months later, caught in a snare set in the park's perimeter fence by local villagers. The fence is supposed to keep deer from ravaging the village crops but poachers had cut holes in it so that the ungulates could be caught as they squeezed through. The little tigress was probably an unintentional victim.

Like most young animals in a litter, cubs develop a sort of pecking order between themselves. You can observe this in action for yourself if you are lucky enough to see cubs at a kill. Adult tigers almost always eat one at a time, even when gathered to feed on a large kill, but cubs often pile in together for a meal and the dominant one is usually the one that gets nearest to the rump. If the tigress is not feeding at this prime location, it will be occupied by the largest cub and the others will fan out away from it. In a large litter, the smallest cub may not get a space at the table until one of the others has finished and, if food is short, this can spell starvation.

Male cubs quickly grow bigger and throw their weight around but they are not necessarily the most adventurous. I have often noticed that female cubs seem less wary and more inclined to investigate weird objects, such as Englishmen on elephants. Curiosity probably depends as much on temperament as on gender. As early as six or seven months, a cub may start wandering off on its own, doing its own sleuthing in the environment, sometimes spending up to 12 hours alone. But at this age it is entirely dependent on its mother for food, so it won't stray far. At 11 or 12 months, cubs begin to get a taste for hunting. They might be able to tackle a chital fawn and, if they live near a village, they may take a goat or a buffalo calf. Schaller

recorded such behaviour in 1964–5 in the male of his Kanha family, which he claimed had been killing small prey for himself from 11 months on and was nearly independent of his mother at 16 months. This male was quite precocious, however, whereas most yearlings are inept.

The bond between siblings can be strong, reinforced by all that play and by the sharing of countless suppers. This bond is valuable because they will probably hunt together for several months after they have left their mother, in effect helping each other to make the transition from a tight family circle to final and solitary independence. This split is not usually a sudden affair but a gradual changing of habits and drifting apart. As the cubs reach 18 or 20 months they are nearly fully grown and are able to hunt for themselves. Indeed, they must do so because a tigress cannot supply a daily diet for such large companions and, since prey is unlikely to be concentrated in just one area of the home range, the cubs eventually have to separate from their mother to find it.

Until they disperse, however, the tigress continues to comfort them with affectionate physical contact. Although they are technically weaned after their first five or six months and her milk dries up, a mother tigress may allow her cubs to suckle her at almost any age. One of the most touching sights I have seen in the wild was a tigress with her two nearly grown cubs in

Bandhavgarh in 2001. She lay half on her side in a grassy clearing while her female cub buried her face in her nipples, softly suckling for half an hour. The huge male cub walked over to them, rubbed faces with his mother and curled up at the back of her head like a vast striped pillow, and then opened his mouth in a wide yawn of absolute comfort. He already had his massive canine teeth – and so probably did his smaller sister. But tigers can obviously be gentle if they want to be and there was certainly no indication that the burrowing female cub was annoying or discomforting her mother.

There can be no doubt that the members of a tiger family derive solace from each other. They like to flop down beside one another, flanks or paws touching, and the sight of a pile of tigers is often a picture of contentment without edge or menace. Mother and cubs are always aware of each other, responsive and affectionate. These bonds must eventually dissolve but it requires urgent stimuli – a local shortage of food and the mother coming into oestrus – to achieve the break. Intriguing light was shed on this process of dissolution by the film *Danger in Tiger Paradise*. Just before the tigress Maachli left her two 17-month-old male cubs to mate with Nick, her new young male, she was filmed suckling them. They were both almost fully grown and already a lot bigger than she was, so what was she doing? According to the film-team, this was probably the last time the family was seen together. Was she comforting them? Is it conceivable, as Valmik Thapar suggests in his commentary, that this was a final farewell before the cubs set out on their journey towards solitary adulthood? Or is it possible that a seemingly unambiguous indication of bonding can also carry a more subtle message? Was she, for instance, with such late dry suckling, reinforcing the fact that their childhood was over and it would soon be time to move on? Or was she just coming into oestrus and feeling broody? Or was she reinforcing for Nick the fact that they were still cubs? Clearly, we still have much to learn about tigers.

The transient life

As the tigress comes into oestrus and mates again, it is the beginning of the end of family life for her cubs. For one thing, an adult resident male will be hanging around regularly now and he may not tolerate the cubs, especially if they are males and even if he is their father – which is statistically unlikely anyway, given the short average breeding life of adult males. Furthermore, the tigress may produce a new litter of cubs within three or four months and then she will actively drive her old cubs away. At around 20–24 months the cubs will be on their own, moving as transients through the jungle they thought was home. This is the second most dangerous time of their lives. According to Ullas Karanth, transients suffer an average annual mortality rate of 30–35 per cent. This compares with just 5 per cent for breeding females and 15 per cent for breeding males. They get into fights with larger residents and other transients, and because they are often forced out to peripheral habitat close to farmland and villages, they are likely to get poisoned by angry farmers whose cattle they have attacked or be killed by poachers. The survivors are the ones that develop the skill of invisibility. They learn to read the signs left by larger, more aggressive tigers so that they can avoid them. They lie low, hunting by night in the areas of other tigers' ranges that are temporarily out of use or where the dominant tiger passed through a day or two previously.

When the Ranthambhore tigress Maachli's two male cubs dispersed in late January 2001, they completely disappeared. One of them had a conspicuous kink in his tail so he was easy to recognize but no one spotted either him or his brother. After several months the film-crew thought they must have died or wandered out of the park – and outside Ranthambhore there is really nowhere safe to go. Then one day in early summer they

Opposite: Youngsters may be injured or killed by other tigers when they start to search for a home range.

found the carcass of a nilgai. It had not been killed by a tiger but it had the prints of a young male all round it. There was no water, no shade, no sign of the tiger and the temperature was 40°C (104°F). There was a small ruined building nearby but they decided not to use it, waiting instead in the open all day in the hope that the young tiger might return to the carcass and turn out to be one of the cubs. Eventually they heard a tiger cough; it was in the building. The next morning when they saw it, they identified it as Broken Tail (see photo pp. 52–53). He had only moved 1.4 km (¾ mile). By hiding and scavenging he had successfully negotiated the first difficult months of his independence without anyone knowing he was there – including perhaps the other tigers.

For a young male, this hole-and-corner existence may last for several years. Dominant males can be hard to shift. Even when he is injured, a resident tiger has the benefit of age, experience and close knowledge of his hunting grounds to aid him, and his powers of recovery can be prodigious. Karanth recorded a male in Nagarahole that was terribly scarred by a huge shoulder wound but that held on to his range for three years after sustaining the injury. Another lost an ear in a fight and ended up with a severe limp yet lived on for two more years.

As we will see, young females have an easier time. They are able to network with their relatives in the neighbourhood and, if they are sufficiently adept to survive those first lonely months, they will probably carve out some sort of range for themselves as soon as they are ready to breed. In some cases the networking can be surprisingly active. Raghu Chundawat has recorded two young sisters in Panna – both radio-collared – teaming up with each other again after a period of solitary dispersal to oust another female from the range.

What exactly do we mean by territory?

Are tigers strictly territorial?

How do tigers leave messages for each other?

What does the marking fluid consist of?

Do tigresses live in dispersed 'prides'?

Why are males' home ranges much bigger than females'?

How does male behaviour influence tiger productivity?

What really makes male tigers fight each other?

Just how solitary are tigers?

Solitary or Sociable?
How the Tiger Holds Its Kingdom

Here is a quote: 'We have four categories of data that indicate that tigresses are territorial. These include **1** essentially non-overlapping ranges; **2** scent-marking behavior; **3** strong site fidelity; and **4** aggressive behavior between females.'

Here is another: 'There was no evidence of territorial behavior in tigresses at Kanha, and they readily shared their range with each other and with the male.'

And another: 'In 82 encounters with tigers either hunting or just walking along, two adults were together in just two instances; the others were solitary animals or tigresses accompanied by one or more young.'

And yet another: 'Nine tigers surround us at varying distances from the nilgai. Hardly daring to breathe, our eyes switch from tiger to tiger ... Four are sleeping, two are grooming, and two are watching the kill. One is on its back, paws in the air.'

The first quote is taken from a scientific paper by Dave Smith, Charles McDougal and Mel Sunquist. The second and third are by George Schaller and the fourth is Valmik Thapar. All have impeccable credentials yet at first glance they seem to be contradicting each other. Tigresses are territorial. No, they are not. Tigers are solitary. No, they are not. So are some of our experts right and the others complete idiots? Of course not. What these quotes reveal is not the fallibility of scientists but the sheer complexity of tiger behaviour.

The traditional view of the tiger, derived mainly from the writings of hunters and pre-war naturalists, has been that it is a solitary, unfriendly beast that inhabits its own fiercely defended territory and comes together only to mate. The contrast was often made with lions, which lived their lives in jolly family groups, sharing bed and board, and in a general sense this was correct. But modern studies have shaded in the detail, revealing the tiger to be an animal whose solitariness is dictated more by environment than by temperament and whose social structures may be more like the lion's than we previously thought.

What do we mean by territory?

Let's look first at the question of territory. By territory we mean something quite distinct from home range. A home range is a geographical area of the landscape where a particular animal is most likely to be found but which is not necessarily defended and

may be shared with others. A territory is exclusive: a patch of land with defined boundaries over which other members of the same species step at their peril. It is a little like the difference between your home town and your home. In your home town you know your way around, do your shopping, say hello to acquaintances. But your home is private. You feed and care for your own family there and if you came down in the morning to find your neighbours sprawling with a picnic on your lawn, 'hello' might not comprise the sum total of your communication.

Different species of animal exhibit different types of territorial behaviour and it is worth looking at a variety of these to see where tigers fit in. The Indian rhino is not territorial yet it is capable of extreme aggression. Rhinos share home ranges, join each other amicably in wallows and even use communal latrines. But they seem to have a need for personal space. Away from the wallows – which are in short supply and therefore not practical to fight over – they keep a distance of roughly 30 m (100 feet) from each other. If another rhino looks like getting closer than that they raise their heads and stare, then give out a warning snort. A female with a calf or a dominant male will attack if further encroached upon. Males fight each other when a female comes into oestrus but she is the stimulus for battle, not any sort of territorial line. So aggression alone is not a defining feature of territoriality.

Even closely related species of animal inhabiting roughly the same terrain can exhibit a wide variety of territorial behaviour. Perhaps the best studied are the East African antelopes, which may live side by side but have completely different life strategies. I have often watched a male impala, for instance, standing still under a tree at the heart of his small territory during the

Opposite: African antelopes show many different types of territorial behaviour.

breeding season. This territory is rarely more than a couple of hundred metres long and will usually have shade and good grazing with which he hopes to tempt groups of females. But if another male encroaches, he bounces out, chasing him off with a nod and a shake of his horns. Sometimes he has to fight and all the bouncing and fencing mean that after a few weeks he loses condition. He will then be ousted by another dominant male, at which point he rejoins a bachelor herd for rest and recuperation before trying for another territory.

Thomson's gazelles and wildebeest, on the other hand, carry their territories with them. As the herds move across the Serengeti Plains they take up stances – all evenly spaced out as if on separate 'plates'. They prance and show off and head-butt their neighbours while the females feed around them, and are occasionally sufficiently excited to mate. As the herd moves, most of the males pack up their 'plates' and move with them. Under such nomadic circumstances it would be impractical to keep establishing and defending large territories, so only a tiny ring of land suffices. Some males, however, usually in prime grazing areas, remain behind to take up arms in the same place at the same time the following year.

Then there are the biggest and the smallest antelope, the eland and the dik-dik, which have entirely opposite strategies. Dominant male elands are solitary. They develop a distinctive outline, with a large goitre on the neck and a tuft of hair that sticks forward above the eyebrows, and the ligaments in their knees click loudly. This clicking is audible over several kilometres and their outline is visible in open ground over large distances. Consequently, mature males need never bother each other and rarely fight. Hierarchies may well already have been established between them during the years they spent together in bachelor herds, so these need not be tested by further aggression. Mature males have small home ranges, while females wander over hundreds of square kilometres in hen-party herds containing

wilderness quality of their environment, dik-diks live rather suburban lives, each little family being separated by clearly defined and defended boundaries. Dik-diks are supreme gardeners. They know every plant in their allotment and they prune them continuously – a nibble here, a nibble there – to ensure that the plants are maintained in good condition and never overgrazed. This horticultural skill is essential because they must derive all their water needs as well as their nutrition from their plot. Intruders don't appreciate the lay-out of the plot and have less interest in conservation, so the male dik-dik keeps them at bay with an elaborate display of energetic shadow-boxing, though this rarely escalates to a contact sport. Dik-diks are very charming. They appear to mate for life and a bereaved male has been known to fend off the attentions of an eligible replacement mate for months at a time.

Other territorial strategies

Although these examples are from East Africa, the different strategies – the interchangeable territory, the portable territory, the solitary life, the allotment – add to our understanding of how variable territoriality can be. Sadly, there are no such aggregations of antelopes in any part of the tiger's range but ungulates are still plentiful and I recall one almost African experience in Kaziranga. There is a beautiful lake far inside the closed core of the park that tourist vehicles cannot reach and where I used to go to film what I thought of as a touch of paradise. One February afternoon I was tucked into the long grass by the edge of the wide marsh that spreads down to the lakeside. The late sunshine was casting the line of bombax trees behind the lake into rich silhouette and the flocks of bar-headed geese were restive, honking and rising to wheel round and land again up and down the shore, practising for their coming journey north to Russia. Rhinos, herds of buffalo and gangs of small red hog deer

dozens – sometimes hundreds – of animals coming to the males when they want them.

For the plains and grasslands herbivores, food is plentiful, so territoriality is about mating rights and not grazing rights. For the little dik-dik, however, this is not the case. If you drive carefully through the dry bush country you can spot the dik-diks, tucked one at a time under bushes, their large dark eyes, reddish side-stripes and, on the males, tiny pointy horns, the only visible features of grey fur against a grey background. You don't see herds of dik-diks. Father, mother and baby form the largest aggregation you are likely to find. Why? Because the unappealing habitat in which they have carved out their modest niche often contains little food and no water. Consequently, despite the

dotted the lakeside. In the water 40 barasingha, wading up to their knees, sieved the waterweeds through their teeth, the spray gushing and sparkling from their mouths, and then a herd of 20 elephants stepped into the open. One by one they filed past me, 3 m (10 feet) away, their great legs framing the scene of lake and ungulate bliss beyond. The story nearly ended in tears. The last elephant stopped short of me, raised her trunk and opened her ears. Very gingerly, bent double, I tried to sneak back to the jeep but she turned and strode towards me. I reached the jeep and

Opposite: The dik-dik prunes every plant in its 'garden' with great care.

Above: Some wildebeest carry their 'territory' with them even when they are on the move.

rolled into the back just as the driver took off. The rough terrain meant that we could only limp away. Behind us the elephant came on, trunk raised, walking fast. She kept pace with us for over 1 km (½ mile), until we reached the main track and she decided we were off her patch. She wasn't being territorial so much as defending her family.

A year earlier, working for the BBC series *Land of the Tiger*, I had the chance to film two other quasi-territorial strategies. The first involved the courtship display of barasingha at Kishanpur in Uttar Pradesh. These deer lived in the middle of a swamp and the dominant males took it in turns to commandeer a small wallow on the edge of long grass, where they could hide from tigers or each other. The wallowing male would roll in the wet dip, coating

himself in black mud so that he looked dark and menacing. He would then dig up the mud with his antlers, piling dead grass and earth on them to increase his impressiveness. Finally, he would walk up onto a little mound behind the wallow, from where he would look out for likely females. If he was lucky, a female, attracted by his grand appearance, would saunter past the mound, luring him down to follow her nose-to-tail until, with a brief jump and buck of the hips, he mounted her. Possession of the wallow and the mound was clearly of paramount importance but I only saw young deer fighting for it. As soon as a really mature male moved towards it or even looked at them, the younger males would vacate it. I never saw a senior male challenged or two senior males together either on the mound or in the wallow. They may have fought at night. I arrived each

morning before dawn; sometimes I heard sounds of conflict in the dark and some of the stags carried visible injuries. In this case the 'territory' was a feature of ritual significance rather than a more generalized resource and, perhaps because mounds in a swamp are in short supply, the males had to take it in turns to use it.

An amusing incident occurred as I was filming this sequence. There was a watch-tower 2 km (1¼ miles) away from which one could monitor my part of the swamp and where my assistant kept guard when I was in the hide. One afternoon we were checking the area and heard the distant alarms of the deer. Their heads were all turned towards the far-off fringe of elephant grass and, after scouring up and down with our binoculars, we finally spotted a tiger. It had its back to us and was watching the deer as intently as they were watching it. The only part of it we

could really see were the two white spots on the back of its black ears. The next morning I was back in my hide among the deer when the alarms began to bark out again. This time they were staring at a clump of grass opposite me and several females bounced away from it, clearly terrified. I focused on the patch and waited excitedly for the tiger. What emerged, however, was a haystack. A show-off of a stag had piled so much grass on his head that his girlfriends couldn't see what he was. Worse still, he couldn't see either. He had no idea where he was going and blundered blindly round the swamp until all his friends had cleared off. I thought there might be a message here for overly ambitious bodybuilders and chaps who drive sports cars.

The second territorial sequence that I filmed showed the mating habits of the blackbuck. Blackbuck are one of only five species of antelope in India. They are quite small, about 75 cm (30 inches) at the shoulder and extremely beautiful. They all have pure-white throats and bellies but the adult males are jet black on head and back, with startling white eye patches and long spiralled horns, while the females and young males are brown. I filmed them against the buffs and yellows of the dry grass plains of Velavader in Gujarat. There the rut occurs in February. I set up my hide in the middle of the rutting field, a short-grass meadow where the dominant males came every morning and evening to stand. They each had their own pitch about 10 m (33 feet) apart, and at its centre was the owner's proudest boast – a big pile of his own dung pellets. Combative neighbours would stalk on stiff legs, side by side, up and down their little boundaries, heads turned slightly away from each other. Then suddenly they would wheel and lock horns in fights that could last several minutes. Most of the time, however, they

Opposite: A barasingha makes its silhouette look more impressive by putting grass on its antlers.
Above: Male blackbucks defend their own patches of dung.

just stood, or lay by their dung piles, occasionally anointing dead grass stems with the secretions from their round cheek glands. Males were allowed across the meadow at the start and end of sessions if they had a pile of their own to go to but if they were not property owners they had to run or risk attack. Females in heat would walk into the meadow to sniff the dung piles and, apparently, to choose a mate, who would then follow her off to the taller grasses beyond for a circular dance that might end in a short stab of love. As the morning wore on and the temperature rose, the bucks would get tired and gradually straggle off the battlefield to feed, returning for the late afternoon and remaining on pitch all night. The whole event was like a sort of mating fair, with the orderly disposition of the males resembling tents pitched on a field. For me, one of the charms was that the dung piles attracted insects and so were constantly picked over by flocks of short-toed larks. Sometimes these were chased in sweeping circles over the tawny grasses by keen pallid harriers and Montagu's harriers, the males flashing silver in the sunlight. In the evening the harriers would glide in to roost on the ground, dozens of them dotted among the blackbucks, while jackals would lope hopefully across the meadow, calculating the chances of getting a harrier for dinner. After a few weeks, the rut packs up, the meadow is deserted and the males and females go back to their separate herds.

Another interesting aspect of territorial behaviour is the 'psychological' confidence boost that an animal enjoys from being in its own territory. In a battle it seems that possession is nine-tenths of the victory. In the 1960s Jane Goodall and Hugo van Lawick studied and filmed spotted hyenas in the Ngorongoro Crater in Tanzania. The walls of the crater are 400 m (1300 feet) high and since there are 300 sq km (116 square miles) of grazing at the bottom – give or take a salt lake and a marsh or two – the herds of gazelle and buffalo and the numerous families of zebra stay there all year round. For the hyenas this means a more or less constant food supply, and Dr Hans Kruuk had already discovered that they had carved the crater floor into separate territories, each one owned and patrolled by whole clans. The clans were extended families ruled by an alliance of dominant females, and teams went out every day to leave trails of scent marks along the boundaries of each clan's territory. Consequently, the lines of demarcation were very specific – this rock was inside the 'Scratching Rocks Clan' property, that one was on 'Lakeside' land – and any infringement by either side was fiercely resisted. The invisible line itself was important. One evening Goodall and van Lawick noticed that two 'Lakesiders' had carelessly fallen asleep just inside enemy territory. Suddenly an advance party of 'Scratching Rockers' arrived and tore into them. One escaped but the other was engulfed in a sea of enemy jaws. Moments later a rescue party of 'Lakesiders' arrived. They were pushed back into their own territory but there they took heart and, though outnumbered, chased the 'Scratching Rockers' back over the line. More and more hyenas joined in the fray until there were between 30 and 40 on each side. For 20 minutes the two clans rolled back and forth over the frontier, advancing or retreating depending on whether they were within or outside their line of confidence. This was the ultimate territorial dispute – a fight over a piece of land provoked apparently by simple trespass. Most fights are likely to involve an intruder's attempt to appropriate a resource, be it food or a female in oestrus. This one was about real estate.

It is worth noting here that this sort of conflict would be unlikely to occur 50 km (30 miles) north, up on the Serengeti Plains. There the herds of ungulates move in a slow clockwise circle round an area upwards of 20,000 sq km (7720 square miles). The hyenas may rely more on scavenging than they do in the crater and their territorial behaviour is more fluid and heterogeneous. So even within a single species the system of land tenure can vary according to the conditions.

Before leaving the general subject of territoriality I should mention the work of David Lack. In 1943 he wrote a seminal work on animal behaviour called *The Life of the Robin*. By a characteristic stroke of genius he used a common and familiar bird to illustrate the new scientific thinking about what makes animals tick. Robins are notoriously territorial, but in his summary of what was then known, Lack pointed out a number of confusing discrepancies. Robin territories varied in size even where the conditions appeared similar. Most territories were bigger than food requirements would dictate yet some robins chose to collect food from beyond their own boundaries. Finally, British robins reasserted their boundaries by singing in the autumn, even though they might not maintain them in the winter. In this last instance Lack posited a theory that autumnal singing was triggered by a hormonal response that 'reminded' the bird not to migrate. Continental robins move south in the winter but the British climate makes this unnecessary. Perhaps natural selection has ensured that British robins that inherited the autumnal hormonal urges to sing survived better than those who migrated. In other words, this was territorial behaviour that had nothing to do with territory. Lack was the director of the Edward Grey Institute for Field Ornithology in Oxford. The questions that he asked have kept two generations of scientists busy, including, for instance, extensive studies of great tits in Wytham Wood.

Among many other things, the Wytham studies showed that, as nest holes and food availability increased towards the centre of the wood, so territory sizes declined. This, as we shall see, has considerable relevance to tigers.

So what have we learnt from this survey of territorial behaviour in various animals? Firstly, that territory is a complicated issue. Territories can be temporary parade grounds for attracting mates; they can be small permanent food resources for the nuclear family; or extensive estates shared by the related members of a clan. They can vary in size and purpose even within individuals of the same species. They can be delineated by display, by scent-marking and by audio stimuli like the robin's song. The boundaries can be flexible, approximate or precise and defended by mock fights or fatal encounters.

Finally, they can be resource-based or just a means by which members of a species are evenly spaced throughout the available habitat. Where, then, among all this variety, does the tiger fit?

How the tiger marks its range

In November 1997 my friend Druv Singh and I followed a tiger on his scent-marking tour through the forest of Kishanpur. We had been filming all day and it was an hour after dark when the tiger pulled in front of us on the track. Though we did not wish to disturb him, he was using our only exit route so we had a fair excuse for staying on his tail. He was entirely indifferent to the lights of our jeep and meandered along about 20 m (65 feet) ahead, sniffing the vegetation on the right-hand side. He never walked off to the left, where tall trees grew right to the edge of the track. Every 100 m (320 feet) or so he would stop, turn into the straggly bushes to the right, smell them, rub his face in them and then reverse, lift his tail and squirt their leaves with what appeared to be urine. The jet shot up at a slight angle, soaking the leaves about 1.5 m (5 feet) above the ground. Sometimes he

would mark a tree trunk rather than a bush and all the marking points were about 20 m (65 feet) off the track, just at the line where the low vegetation merged into the line of full canopy trees. We followed him for more than half an hour and all that time he seemed quietly preoccupied – calm, slow, relaxed, but purposeful. Where the track eventually emerged from the trees it crossed a railway line and, as if recognizing this as a frontier or an obstacle, about 100 m (320 feet) short of it the tiger turned abruptly off to the right, stopped scent-marking and disappeared slowly into the pitch darkness of the deep forest.

In many ways this was a typical tiger sighting. Any observer who has watched tigers for a while will have dozens of similar experiences recorded in his or her notebooks. Tigers, both males and females, spend a lot of time scent-marking and the fluid is probably not merely urine. Back in 1967 George Schaller noticed that it smelled 'very musky', much stronger than normal urine, and that it was discernible even to the human nose at a distance of 3–5 m (10–16 feet). The 'marking fluid' has since been studied by two scientists, R. L. Brahmachary and J. Dutta (in *Tigers of the World*), who have found that, though its base is uric acid, the more exciting scents are probably carried in some of the other components of the fluid, including chemicals like phenylethylamine, cadaverine and putrescine. Somewhere in there are pheromones, the chemicals that stimulate animals in their sexual activities. When a tiger smells the fluid – either its own or someone else's – it will often wrinkle its nose and pull its lips away from its teeth in a conspicuous grimace that scientists call 'flehmen'. This is the same face that stallions pull when they scent a mare in oestrus and that antelopes and deer make as they sniff the bottom of a receptive female. It is now believed that the grimace transfers the scent to a hitherto little understood part of the nose called Jacobson's organ. Recent studies have shown that this little organ is wired to the part of the brain that interprets tastes rather than smells. In other words, flehmen permits the tiger, whose sense of smell is active but not powerful, to 'taste' a scent as well as smell it.

The information gathered is probably quite detailed, providing a sort of chemical profile of the tiger that left the scent: its individual identity, its age and sex, possibly its status as a dominant or transient animal, its overall health and the state of its hormones. A female in oestrus will leave a very strong message and this is probably answered by an equally strong one from an eligible male. In an environment where it may be difficult or undesirable for tigers to meet, the lines of scent marks act as a bulletin board, a sort of Internet system among animals that may wish to know all about each other without coming face to face.

Of itself, scent-marking is not an automatic indication of territorial behaviour. All tigers do it sometimes, both residents and transients. Females do it more when they are in oestrus and

males are even more active when an oestrus female is around. There is no doubt, then, that the simple bulletin element – 'Here I am, I'm feeling sexy' or 'This is me and I'm big and dangerous' or just 'Here I am, I won't be staying' – is very important. Indeed, tigers leave all sorts of messages for each other. The simple act of depositing faeces is usually a statement. Faeces are often left in a conspicuous position, like the grass centre of a forest track, and anointed with a smelly secretion from the anal gland. Sometimes tigers place their faeces and urine on the bare soil of a scrape mark. They dig out these scrapes with their hind feet – thrusting backwards, usually to leave two parallel marks about 30 cm (12 inches) long. Schaller made an interesting observation in Kanha, finding more dung in scrapes during and after the monsoon when the soil was damp. He suggested that in the wet season dung beetles make a speedy job of removing or covering

faeces, so the scrape draws attention to the dung site even if the dung is not easily visible. Passing tigers will then investigate the scrape and smell the telltale faecal residue. In the dry season the faeces harden quickly and remain as landmarks for weeks, so the scrape – less visible in any case in the baked soil – is less useful.

Tigers have definite strategies for ensuring that their marks last for as long as possible. On my first walk with Dave Smith in Chitwan I remember him pointing out a scent mark on the underside of a sloping tree. The patch was several days old but still damp and musky. The slope of the trunk acted as a roof, protecting the stain from the hot rays of the sun and from washing away in the rain, thereby giving it days – perhaps weeks – of extra potency. A 'long-life' mark saves energy because it means that the owner does not have to tramp round renewing its signs as frequently as it would if they faded quickly. Ullas Karanth thinks this may also be why tigers sometimes flick earth and leaves over their faeces – not to hide them but to conserve them – though this may just be an accidental result of reflex scraping.

There is one other more or less permanent mark that tigers make. They stand against a tree on their hind legs, reaching up at almost full stretch, and pull their claws down the trunk, leaving deep rakes in the surface. Sloth bears do the same and it is generally assumed that the action helps to clean and sharpen their claws, though its efficacy has not been studied. Large tigers presumably leave scratches further up the trunk, so perhaps the tree acts as a sort of measuring gauge: 'Watch out, look how far he can reach.' We don't really know but it is my impression that tigers have favourite scratching trees – they certainly reuse them – and opt for those with medium-hard trunks: trees like the fruit-bearing mahua (*Madhuca indica*) or arjuna (*Arjuna termenalia*),

Opposite: Tiger smelling scent-mark sprayed on the underside of a tree.
Above: The author examining scratchmarks left more than 2 m (6 feet) up a tree trunk.

which are soft enough to receive a mark but not so soft as to leave the tiger with a handful of wood chippings between its nails. I have never seen scratch marks on sal, which is a very hard wood. The joy of scratching also seems to vary from tiger to tiger. In Bandhavgarh there have been three brothers in recent years who live adjacent to each other and all of whom seem to be keen scratchers, especially the one known as B2. Very often when I get the chance to follow him along a track, I see him stop for a quick scratch at a tree. Yet a couple of hundred kilometres away in Kanha, in the mid-1960s, Schaller didn't find a single lacerated tree, so presumably the tigers in his study area at that time were not enthusiasts.

Finally, there is one other obvious bulletin that a tiger can issue. It can roar. Tigers do not roar very often and this fact alone is probably a clue to the nature of their social life. Lions (particularly lionesses) are very vocal. The typical roar, followed by a descending series of roaring grunts, is a way for pride members to keep in touch with each other in the dark or initiate an assembly. One evening in Gujarat I was watching a lioness who had spent the whole afternoon dozing in a clearing on top of a hill in the scrub forest of Gir. As the heat went out of the day and the sun reddened, she stood up and roared, receiving a prompt but distant answer. She lay down again and about ten minutes later an adult offspring, probably three years old, walked out from under the trees and rubbed her face over her mother's neck. Five minutes later a second lioness arrived. They all greeted each other, lay down together for some minutes and then left the clearing, probably to start hunting.

A tiger family with such grown-up young would already have split up, but until they do so, mother and cubs are rarely far apart and so while moans and grunts and warning coughs between them are frequent, long-range signalling is not, unless it is accomplished by the use of low-frequency sounds (see below). Most of the time tigers, it would seem, have no one to talk to. The roar itself is a huge sound which, as we have seen, is apparently capable of terrifying everything in the jungle. One would think it would make a very effective territorial signal. Tawny owls in an English woodland inhabit year-round constant territories and maintain them by their characteristic long-range hooting. So why don't tigers do the same with their magnificent roar? One answer seems to be that they keep it in reserve for something more important to them: mating. An intriguing piece of recent research, however, suggests tigers may have another way of communicating. In the 3 May 2003 issue of *New Scientist* Ed Walsh and colleagues from the Boys Town National Research Hospital in Omaha, Nebraska, USA, described the tiger's use of low-frequency booming sounds at levels below 20 hertz which would be

inaudible to humans. So perhaps there is more chat going on out there than we think.

All these tiger signs can potentially have two meanings, either as warnings or advertisements: 'I'm here, so keep away' or 'I'm here, come and find me.' The strongest proof that they can be used as territorial markings rather than merely personal spacing mechanisms comes from the Chitwan study. Between January 1974 and June 1985 the Smithsonian/Nepal team had 11 radio-collared tigresses under observation. This meant that by daily tracking of the individual radio signals emitted by each collar they knew precisely where each tigress was and could build up a very accurate picture of their land usage. They discovered that their tigresses were using mutually exclusive areas of the Chitwan forest and that their scent-marking activity increased in frequency the closer they came to the notional borders. Raghu Chundawat has more recently observed the same pattern of increase among male and female tigers in Panna.

Tigresses as range-holders

Other fascinating revelations emerged from the tigress part of the Chitwan study – the entire study dealt with males and females and the complete ecology of the species. Firstly, in all, they followed 14 females that they believed to be 'territorial'. Of these, 13 had at least one litter of cubs within their 'territories'. The fourteenth was tranquillized and shifted from the park after she killed a man. This indicated that, for females, a 'territory' was primarily a breeding space – only required as a safe haven in which to give birth and raise cubs. Secondly, the pattern of tenure showed that the females in any area tended to be related to each other. Diagrams of the process by which daughters moved out of the maternal range to settle next door, or even within a

Opposite: A tiger in its own range can be completely relaxed.

ceded portion of it, resemble neat pictures of cell division. By spring 1986 the team had documented no fewer than 13 pairs of neighbours that were also relatives. This confirmed what Schaller had partially suspected – that tigers were much more like lions than was generally believed. Tigresses settled the land like a pride of lions (prides being groups of related females and their cubs), but a dispersed pride that never actually lived together.

Lionesses live in prides because in their relatively open landscapes a successful hunter is quickly spotted by others and, unless she can defend her kill, she will be robbed. In most seasons prey is sufficiently plentiful for lions not to need help in hunting. What they do need is help with hanging on to their dinners. They have enough to do keeping hyenas at bay without having to fight each other as well, so they have evolved a pride system that involves sharing kills. Tigers are very closely related to lions and probably share some of their social genes. But in their thicker forest environment, kills are not as conspicuous and prey not as concentrated, so it is neither necessary nor practical to live as prides. It is, however, practical to share out the wider landscape with the minimum of fighting and this is naturally achieved by settling next to relatives. The downside is that genetic variety is diminished but this problem is addressed by the males, which have been shown to disperse further than females and are statistically less likely to settle next to close relatives. Again, as with lions, the females concentrate on raising the young as efficiently as possible, while the males mate as frequently and as far away from their birthplace as possible.

The Chitwan study found that the transfer of real estate between females was often the result of a peaceable evolution rather than a sudden conflict. Mel and Fiona Sunquist describe one such change in their popular book *Tiger Moon*. Number 1 tigress (101), the first wild tigress in the world to wear a radio-collar, had lived in the same home range for at least three years. In January 1976 she was forced to move her litter of cubs from her favourite denning area in elephant grass near the Rapti river after being disturbed by grass-cutters. She moved 3 km (1¾ miles) to a distant corner of her territory and, because mothers never hunt far from their very young cubs, she lost touch with the bulk of her range for several months. In that period her grown-up daughter, the 'Roaring Tigress' – so named because she was extremely vocal in her quest for a mate – gradually moved into the untenanted area. Meanwhile, her mother lost her cubs but, though she occasionally returned to her old range, she never regained it. Instead, by early summer, she began to infiltrate the range of her western neighbour, the 'Jarneli Tigress'. According to the Sunquists' account, she and the Jarneli Tigress had lived side by side for two years without ever trespassing on each other's patch. In October the Roaring Tigress bore a litter in exactly the same thicket that her mother, Number 1, had used at least twice previously – bearing out the notion that appropriation of a territory is motivated by the imminent process of mating and producing cubs. Meanwhile, Number 1 settled down on the southern edge of her old range, raising one more litter and living there until she was, sadly, poisoned by villagers three years later.

Such peaceful shifts of ownership probably explain why Schaller found 'no evidence of territorial behavior in tigresses at Kanha'. He did, however, notice that each one had a 'center of activity'. So when does a centre of activity become a territory? We have seen that breeding tigresses establish a more or less exclusive range in which they will raise their cubs and whose boundaries they will mark. What they do not do, and this applies to males as well, is fight over the lines of demarcation in the way that the Ngorongoro hyenas did. No tiger is going to rush across its territory to beat up a rival who has peed on the wrong tree. Fights are almost always about resources – a kill; or, between males, a female in oestrus; or, between male and female, the fate of young cubs (see *Infanticide*, pp. 54–56). Territorial fights do occur, however, and can be serious, but they appear to be motivated by a general conflict over space rather than by any precise infringement of property rights. In their 2000 BBC film *The Tigers' Fortress* Dr Mike Birkhead and cameraman Colin Stafford Johnson recorded a violent battle in Ranthambhore between the young tigress Maachli and her own mother. The mother was displaced, while Maachli went on to retain her mother's old range and produced at least two litters of cubs in it. As an individual, Maachli turned out to be a 'territorial' tigress in quite another sense. Tigresses in oestrus will wander well outside their usual centre of activity in search of a mate. When Maachli came into oestrus, however, she proved nervous of foreign travel, exhibiting a classic loss of confidence outside her own borders. For her first mating she ended up some 3 km (1¾ miles) beyond her own 'frontier'. The film-team tracked her there but she appeared to be so nervous about being on someone else's land that she kept jumping up and looking around as if expecting imminent attack. Not only was the mating unsuccessful, but she ran all the way home, like a guilty teenager, even starting with fear at the alarm calls she was provoking from the terrified sambar she passed on her way. It was not until the male crossed over to her some weeks later that she could settle to mating properly.

So female tigers tend to stake out a home range adjacent or close to that of their own mother. This arrangement is usually friendly and gradual and provides the new young tigress with an unofficial community of neighbours, many of whom are likely to be her relatives – sisters, half-sisters, cousins and aunts. Females do sometimes fight each other and assertive territorial behaviour is more frequent when a tigress becomes a breeding female. Her priority then becomes not merely food but finding and retaining a safe and sufficiently productive place in which she can rear her cubs. It will presumably feel safer if it is exclusive to her. Whether she ends up fighting about it probably depends as much as anything on her own temperament and on that of her neighbours, as well as the degree of kinship she shares with them. In the case of Maachli and her mother, temperament – or a sudden surge of hormonal excitement – overrode the influence of family.

To conclude, all tigresses appear to aspire to be residents in a home range. Most show territoriality when they are mating and rearing cubs, though some more than others, and this simple diversity probably explains why some observers have ascribed overt territorial behaviour to tigresses while others have not.

The life of the male tiger

The mechanics of male behaviour are not so different from that of females. Males too aspire to be resident within a home range, which they mark and patrol in the same way. They too generally avoid conflict and, like the females, when they do fight it is usually over resources rather than boundaries. Where they differ from tigresses is in the resources they most value. Tigresses and tigers are a bit like women and men. To put it crudely, she wants food for the family, he wants sex. Given that all tigers require prey, shade and water, a female's main priority is a suitable place to bring up a litter. A male's main aim in life, however, is to secure access to receptive females. This simple fact explains why the pattern of land tenure among males usually ends up looking so different from that of females. A female needs only one mate. The results of a single mating over five days will keep her busy for two years – the time it takes to rear cubs. She does not require exclusive access, just five days of fun. All she needs is enough space to support the prey required to feed her cubs. These modest needs explain why females can, in evolutionary terms, be less aggressive towards each other. A large territory gives her no added advantage – indeed, she would waste energy defending it.

Above: Siberian male, Gayvoron, Russia.

Consequently, you can have more tigresses in a smaller area, and if they are related to each other they can conserve resources even more efficiently by not fighting with each other and thereby 'helping' to promote related genes. The opposite applies to tigers. Biologically, in the two-year period when a female is occupied with a single litter, a male can sire lots of cubs, so it is in his interests to have the largest possible home range. And this is what happens in practice. The Chitwan study, for instance, found female ranges to be on average only 38 per cent of the size of males' – so whereas female 'territories' varied from 10 to 51 sq km (4–20 square miles) male 'territories' went from 19 up to 151 sq km (8–60 square miles).

Larger territories mean fewer opportunities for young males to settle close to their birth area. This affects male behaviour. Whereas young females may not need to wander, young adult males have to. Biologically, the species requires fewer males and that's what it gets. Because dominant males (unlike females) have no special interest in making room for their sons and brothers, the close relationship pattern applies less to males. Consequently, young tigers meet less tolerance from the resident males in their area and usually end up on the periphery of prime habitats where survival is more difficult. Not surprisingly, male mortality is high. As we have seen, the mortality rate among transients (mostly males) is 30–35 per cent per year. The fact that they have to move is important for another reason. It ensures that genetic diversity is spread further among the population, offsetting any genetic disadvantages that might accrue from the 'pride' effect of adjacent females being related to each other.

As we have seen, male ranges tend to be two to three times larger than those of females, so a dominant resident male will hope to have access to several females on his own doorstep and the status and character of that male will influence the productivity of the tigresses within his range. This is well illustrated by the story of one tiger that Dave Smith told me about in the late 1980s. Put simply, when Smith joined the Smithsonian/Nepal Tiger Ecology Project in Chitwan, he had expected to witness frequent fights between male tigers vying for territory. In fact, in the main study area there was almost no conflict at all. At first the team wondered if they were just failing to observe the correct signs but eventually they realized that two dominant tigers had effectively carved up some 130 sq km (50 square miles) of terrain, containing the ranges of six or seven females, and that, for two years, they rarely trespassed on each other's ranges and never fought. Just when Smith joined the team, however, one of the males, 102 (called the 'Dhakre Tiger' by Charles McDougal), died. At this point Smith predicted an outbreak of warfare as other males made their moves on the vacated territory. But according to Smith, there were still no fights. The remaining male, Tiger 105, simply expanded his own range to take over that of his dead neighbour as well. This tiger had been radio-collared in 1974 and his history was recorded in some detail. He was, apparently, a huge animal weighing some 272 kg (600 lb), so confident that he would walk his favourite paths – even the ridge trail right beside the tourist camp at Tiger Tops – in broad daylight. According to Smith's notes from the time, during the nearly six years that 105 was a dominant resident, he sired no fewer than 51 cubs. Even more astonishingly, 27 of these survived to disperse.

Tiger 105 seems to have achieved this dominance without unnecessary violence. Some six to nine months after 102's death, somewhere between July and December 1977, another, smaller and younger male, Mahala Bhale, settled on the far western edge of what had been 102's but was now 105's range. For the next 13 months, 105 and Mahala Bhale shared this area, even visiting the same bait stations at Tiger Tops, without conflict. Then suddenly, in January 1979, they fought. Trackers found blood in both their spores and Mahala Bhale was walking with a limp. So why the sudden aggression? The answer is that, for the first time since Mahala Bhale had been using that part of 105's new range extension, the local female had come into oestrus. She began calling; Mahala Bhale showed up first and 105 probably caught him with her. Tiger 105 went on to complete the mating process while Mahala Bhale left the area completely.

This incident illustrates the true nature of a tiger's territoriality. A dominant tiger may share part of his range amicably with another male, and as long as they don't keep bumping into each other, he won't get into a fight over bits of land. But there is one resource he values over any other – a female in oestrus. If that comes up for grabs, then woe betide the young pretender.

Tiger 105 died in November 1979. It was then that his true significance became obvious. Like a benign king, his dominant status had provided stability in the area for six years, permitting an unusual number of young tigers, many sired by him, to be born and grow up safely. The early 1980s, by contrast, were years of carnage as untried males competed for the oestrus females. Over a 24-month period, Smith believed that not a single cub from that range made it to adulthood.

In 1992 I made a film entitled *Man-Eater: To Be or Not To Be* for the BBC with Dave Smith and Richard Brock. On the basis of Smith's field notes, we reconstructed the life of another male tiger, Bahadur Bhale. His mother was both a daughter and – because of the sometimes tangled nature of tiger kinship – a granddaughter of 105. He was born in May 1980 and disappeared in August 1988. Aspects of his life are dealt with in *Family Life: The First Months* and *Man on the Menu*, but part of his story is relevant here to the issue of territoriality and breeding success. Like his grandfather, Bahadur Bhale was a powerful tiger, though his route to the top appears to have been much more bloody. According to Smith, he fought at least three other dominant resident tigers, displacing each one from its range until he ended up with six females on his patch. Yet he only managed to mate with four of them and sired only ten cubs, though six of these apparently survived to dispersal, which is a high proportion. So why such a disparity in the performance of Bahadur Bhale and 105? Two factors may just have been bad luck and bad timing. One of his females was very young; another may have been a bit too elderly; and others were occupied with older cubs when he 'inherited' them. A more important reason, however, was that his epoch of maximum stability was much shorter. Although he was a dominant tiger for four and a half years, much longer than average, Bahadur Bhale was still fighting and expanding his range a year before his death. Tiger 105, by contrast, had one and a half more years and was completely stable for most of them. Significantly, his last two years were the most productive, producing 29 cubs. Statistically speaking, 105 sired 56 per cent of his offspring in the final 33 per cent of his period of dominance. This would imply that fighting is bad for productivity and that it is best for the welfare of the species if territorial aggression is kept in check.

The dynamics of tiger distribution

So is the tiger a territorial animal or not? Clearly, tigers don't live in herds. They use scent marks and signs to space themselves out and they will fight each other. But they don't have time for dedicated territorial behaviour. A tiger's patch is too large to be constantly defended, and for an animal that needs to be in tip-top condition just to feed itself, serious fights are best avoided. They are, in fact, quite rare. When they occur they are most likely to be crimes of passion – males fighting over a female. For these reasons it is more satisfactory to describe a tiger as a resident male or female, rather as than as a territory-holder, and to refer to its home range rather than its territory. In his book *The Face of the Tiger* Charles McDougal, one of the most experienced of all tiger observers, says that the process by which ranges are established and delineated boils down to frequency of use. He sums up the general dynamics of tiger distribution very neatly:

In the context of the maintenance of their home ranges by residents, marking lets transients know whether an area is regularly or only irregularly used. The frequency of markers provides a rough index of the intensity of range use and the density of the resident population. A transient searching for a place to settle will not attempt to remain in a place that is already densely populated, unless animals of its own sex are lacking. Rather it will settle where the signs indicate few other tigers, but at the same time the presence of one of the opposite sex.

The relative size of home ranges is one of the few aspects of tiger behaviour that have been extensively studied – and in different parts of Asia. It is one of the most accessible pieces of information that emerges from radio-collaring the animals. All the researchers agree that, while personal character traits – such as the degree of dominance or aggression – may influence the size of an individual tiger's range, the average size of ranges in any area is decided by just one factor: the abundance of prey. So far there have been four outstanding studies. These have been carried out in Chitwan in Nepal by the Smithsonian Tiger Ecology Project; in Nagarahole in southern India by Ullas Karanth; in Siberia's Primorski Krai region by Dale Miquelle, Evgeny Smirnov and others; and most recently in Panna in Madhya Pradesh in central India by Raghu Chundawat.

The results are conclusive and can be simplified as follows: Chitwan and Nagarahole are moist subtropical or tropical forests with riverine grasslands and are rich in prey. Suitable large ungulates exist in densities as high as 60 animals per sq km (⅕ square mile) and range sizes are quite small, on average 10–25 square km (3¾–9½ square miles). Panna occupies the mid-range. It is dry forest with wild ungulates averaging only five per square kilometre but these numbers are swelled by 17.5 cattle per square kilometre. Range sizes consequently turn out to be twice as large, averaging from 30–50 sq km (11½–19 square miles), though sometimes much bigger. Finally, we come to the sparse hillside forests of eastern Siberia, where prey densities can be as low as one or two per square kilometre and ranges can be as extensive as 200 or even 500 sq km (77–193 square miles).

Ullas Karanth has checked these figures using some straightforward mathematics. We know that a tiger requires roughly one large dinner a week. Given that it may mix its meals – a big sambar this week, a huge gaur next week, a couple of small chital over the next ten days – it is fair to say that it needs 50 prey animals per year. To sustain that degree of mortality year in, year out without declining, the population of ungulates in its vicinity needs to be at least ten times as high: say, 500. This means that one tiger needs a herd of 500 ungulates to keep it going. In a place like Nagarahole or Chitwan, where there are at least 50 ungulates per square kilometre, one can calculate that a tiger can find sufficient food within a home range of just 10 sq km

(3¾ square miles) – not far off the real figure. Similarly, in Siberia, with only one ungulate in a square kilometre, a tiger may need 500 sq km (193 square miles) of cold hillside – and again that, it seems, is what it gets.

Although the average sizes of home ranges are influenced by the local abundance of prey, the extremes – the smallest possible range and the largest possible range – are almost certainly governed by social factors. The largest ranges that we are aware of occur in Siberia. There tigers may, exceptionally, roam over 500 sq km (193 square miles). Such a huge expanse must make it difficult for them to meet and mate with each other. Beyond a certain distance, their roars must be inaudible and the chances of picking up scent marks must fade. If the distance separating them becomes too great, individuals will be condemned to eternal solitude and the species to extinction. At the opposite end of the spectrum, Karanth has used camera traps to assess tiger densities in various parts of India and he believes that the highest density occurs on the grassy floodplains of the Brahmaputra river in Kaziranga in Assam. There, he estimated that, including cubs, there might be as many as 20 tigers in a 100-km (62-mile) square and this, he believes, probably represents saturation level. The tiger as we know it has evolved to hunt and live primarily alone, so that scarce resources do not need to be fought over. This it does, as we have seen, by spacing itself out in response to scents and signs. This is instinctive behaviour that has survival value and is unlikely to be overruled by extraordinary conditions. If some phenomenon suddenly produced an infinite number of sambar and chital in Kanha, you would not see an infinite number of tigers there because beyond a certain density the tiger's own behaviour, and not merely its diet, would limit its population. Or would it?

Just as tigers are and are not 'territorial', so they are and are not solitary. Most of the time when you see tigers – unless they are mating or there are cubs involved – you see them alone.

Nevertheless, they have the genes for sociability, so who knows whether, given enough food and enough time, they might not learn to live more closely together? It is probably an idle thought but it does remind us not to take tiger behaviour for granted. I have not yet been lucky enough to see a large gathering of adult tigers but some people have. One of the most spectacular was witnessed by Valmik Thapar and Fateh Singh Rathore in Ranthambhore in November 1982. A dominant tigress they called Padmini killed a 250-kg (550-lb) male nilgai – a very large antelope. They found her at the kill just after dawn with her three 14-month-old cubs and they watched uninterrupted for the next ten hours. During this period the family was joined by two adult females and one adult male – all offspring from Padmini's previous litters and by two unrelated tigers, one female the other unidentified. By three o'clock in the afternoon there were no fewer than nine tigers round the kill. Thapar and Singh saw at least five different tigers eating but never more than one at a time and always, they thought, in an orderly manner controlled by Padmini. Thapar's conclusions are very interesting. He took this event as an indication that tigers recognize the links of kinship long after they are mature and that they can exploit these amicably when a windfall occurs in the form, for instance, of an unusually large kill. If he is correct – and I am convinced that he is – then it is another explanation of why tigers can be so ambiguous in their displays of 'territoriality'. Padmini's nilgai was eaten up in 24 hours and that gathering seems to have been a one-off incident.

In the spring of 1974, however, Charles McDougal watched an assortment of five tigers regularly associating with each other – though never all at once at one kill – at a bait-site near Tiger Tops in Chitwan. They were a mother that he called Kali, her new male friend (but not the father of her cubs), the Amaltari Tiger, her daughter Mohini (aka Bachchi), her son Mohan and his adult female 'friend' Seti. On 59 occasions two or more tigers were seen together and on ten occasions there were four. Again there was a kinship link, through the mother, Kali, between all the tigers. Again there was a dominant tiger, though this time it was the Amaltari male. He, however, proved very 'tolerant' of the others, especially the young male Mohan, whom one might have expected him to resent. But Mohan was a character, a daylight tiger who was usually the first to attack and kill the bait, so he was useful and was often permitted first rights at the food. McDougal was struck by the 'good table manners' exhibited by the tigers. He noted that on those 59 occasions when two or more tigers were together, snarling or other aggressive acts occurred only 12 times; only six times did more than one tiger feed at once, and never two adults together. They took it in turns and always gave each other personal space, keeping 'at least three yards [3 m]' distance. This contrasts with the rough-and-tumble of a lion kill, where the pride members knock each other out of the way in their hurry to cram the food down before it disappears. Good manners, it seems, are a necessary social lubricant among dangerous animals like tigers who, though they may like each other, are forced by circumstances to live most of their lives alone.

Above: Tigresses may share kills with kin (see text p. 89), but if provoked they can become aggressive.

Do adult tigers recognize their own relatives?

Are confined habitats making related tigers less aggressive to each other?

Does less aggression mean more cubs?

Has the real 'wilderness tiger' all but disappeared?

Why do we know so little about the intimate lives of tigers in the past?

Is the Tiger Changing Its Stripes?

Changing Tiger Behaviour

On 26 January 2003 India celebrated Independence Day. At Bandhavgarh the forest department organized a splendid ceremony. We watched hundreds of children from Tala and the surrounding villages – some in school uniform, many with bare feet – as they marched proudly past the flag to receive sticky brown paper packages of sweets. Inside the national park the tigers were probably celebrating too because the gates, which normally open at six in the morning, were still firmly padlocked at a quarter past nine. My companions and I had spent part of the previous day on elephants, climbing high into the hills trying to approach a tigress with four flamboyant cubs. We never reached her.

In the very early mornings the family was usually down in the Chakradhara meadow not far from the park gate. This is a beautiful little valley with stands of silver-topped elephant grass fringed with clear streams. Once the sun had risen, however, and the elephants had begun their patrols and the jeeps had started trundling up and down the valley roads, the tigress would gather her cubs and head for the less accessible uplands.

Independence Day was our last day in the park. Would the tigress be long gone by 9.20 when the gates finally opened or would she have stayed put, enjoying the unaccustomed peace of the morning? Was her behaviour conditioned by us or did she have her own clock? We had an answer within minutes of entering. A warning whistle from another vehicle drew our attention to the first wooded slope beside the meadow and there,

50 m (160 feet) away on a steep, shady incline braced against a tree trunk was a small tiger. Other jeeps stopped. We scoured the shadows for more tigers. The hidden suggestive stripes in clumps of bamboo and behind trees slowly resolved themselves until we could see all four cubs. Then from behind a dark triangle of rock the tigress's head lifted into view.

One by one the cubs crept down the slope to drink from the stream at the bottom. According to Vivek Sharma, who has been monitoring the park's tigers for years, these cubs were born the previous spring so they were now about nine months old. Already the two males could be distinguished by their broader heads and rounder faces. The stream was less than 15 m (50 feet) from us, but where the cubs were, a dense screen of elephant grass blocked our view. We could only imagine what the slurping,

whickering and splashing noises meant and why the tops of the grasses would suddenly heave to right or left. The fourth cub, the smaller of the two little females, was shy and remained up in the woods even when the tigress came to drink. I watched the mother approach, neat and sleek, and as she emerged from the shadows, she looked straight into my binoculars. Her wild eyes filled my view and she flattened her ears and hissed at me. Then I noticed something even more interesting. Back up the slope behind her there was a sixth tiger. It had stood up from somewhere behind the bamboo, or perhaps the mother's rock. It was fully grown but looked very young, in perfect condition, not a hair out of place, not a nick in the ear or scratch on its chin. As it walked away round the edge of the hillside I could see that it was a male.

Now Vivek surprised me. He said the last time he had seen this male had been in early December, when the young tiger had been suckling the tigress. She was not in oestrus and there seemed no question of his being any sort of suitor. Instead, he appeared to be a cub left over from her previous litter, making him 27 months old by this time. As far as we know, it is very unusual for a male cub to remain in his mother's company after she has produced a fresh litter. Even staying within her home range is risky and requires him to keep a very low profile. The new mother does not welcome competition for her cubs' food, or the attentions of any male that is not their father, and if she does not see him off, then the resident male almost certainly will. Vivek had heard the father of both litters – the big tiger B2 – roaring in the area and thought there might have been a one-sided squabble, so he had not expected to see the youngster again. So what was happening?

Opposite: Tigress crouching for a drink.
Above: Female cub still 'suckling' at 17 months – this is
probably a way of saying 'I still need mother's protection'.

In the absence of any true scientific data – no DNA, no radio-collars, no precise minute-by-minute observation – we can only speculate. Given these provisos, this is our interpretation: the young tiger is staying with his mother because he can find nowhere else to go. Dispersal from small reserves like Bandhavgarh is difficult, so the impetus to leave would have to be compelling. For some reason it is not. Neither of the resident adults seems to have put much pressure on this cub and in the meantime he is very self-effacing. By suckling his mother he is saying that he is still a cub, represents no threat and is still in need of her protection. For their part, the adults are tolerating this infantile behaviour because their own aggressive instincts have become softened – a pattern that has arguably been discernible among the tigers of Bandhavgarh for some years.

Bandhavgarh's most famous tiger was called Charger. He was given this name because he liked chasing jeeps. At any time of the day he might come bounding out of the bushes and bounce a vehicle. Headlights in the evening were a great lure and the genes are still there: one of his offspring, the tigress Mohini (aka Bachchi), used to let fly occasionally. Sometimes she bounced the occasional bicycle as well. (Sadly, she seems to have been hit by a car in March 2003 and subsequently disappeared.) Charger died in September 2000. He was 17 years old and very decrepit. This is a

huge age for a male tiger. Normally, as his strength wanes, a resident male loses a fight to a younger rival and either dies of his wounds or slowly starves in exile. Charger was a very dominant tiger but, even though at the end he was being fed by the forest staff, he could never have survived for so long if the males that replaced him had wanted him dead. He did get into fights, he lost and he faded, but they did not actually kill him. Why? Presumably because none of them had successfully dispersed, they were closely related to him, had been tolerated by him and were now, in effect, returning the compliment.

In a confined space – like a small reserve from which there is no easy exit – we might expect animals to become increasingly aggressive. Among rats in a cage, or human beings in crowded cities, we believe we detect a rise in violent behaviour, but this may not apply to tigers. In particular, this assumption may misunderstand the role of genes. We interpret infanticide among tigers as the subordination of the interests of the species to the claims of the 'selfish gene'. A tiger will kill another tiger's cubs so that he can the sooner sire cubs of his own. But if those cubs are

Above: Tigers in parks, like 'B2' in Bandhavgarh, have become used to vehicles.
Opposite: A suggested family tree of some of the tigers in the Tala range, Bhandhavgarh.

already closely related to him – his father's or his brother's – and if, because he and his relatives have continued to rub shoulders together in the same confined space, he knows that, then he might not kill them. In that case the gene also predominates over the purely selfish desires of the individual. As a tiger, his mating opportunities may be denied, but as his genes will survive it doesn't matter.

In small reserves like Ranthambhore, Bandhavgarh and Panna, where the buffer zones are thin and the corridors of dispersal restricted, observers are seeing fewer cases of infanticide and fewer fatal fights between adult tigers. Although Ranthambhore may possibly have a higher turnover of males than the other parks, this is most likely due to extraneous mortality rather than competition. A glance at the family tree (opposite page) of the tigers we see in the Tala range at Bandhavgarh shows how very closely related to each other they all are. What this will do for the bloodstock in the long run is anyone's guess. In the meantime, the heart of the park is shared by three brothers (grandsons of Charger) and there is no doubt that their tolerance of each other and of each other's cubs, and the stability ensured by their peaceable presence, is very good for productivity. When I visited in January 2003 there were three females with a total of ten well-grown cubs, all co-existing within a radius of a few miles.

Even in Kanha there are indications of a change in tiger behaviour. Kanha is a large park. With its buffer zones and associated forest land it covers some 3000 sq km (1160 square miles). Tigers are more free to move around from range to range there and males can disperse over a wider area. Whether or not this mobility is the reason, Kanha tigers have a reputation for violence. Infanticide was widely publicized by Chip Houseman's beautiful BBC film in the late 1990s and there have been regular observations of males killing each other and even killing females. Nevertheless, in the spring of 2002, Naresh Bedi, a very experienced film-maker, made the extraordinary observation of

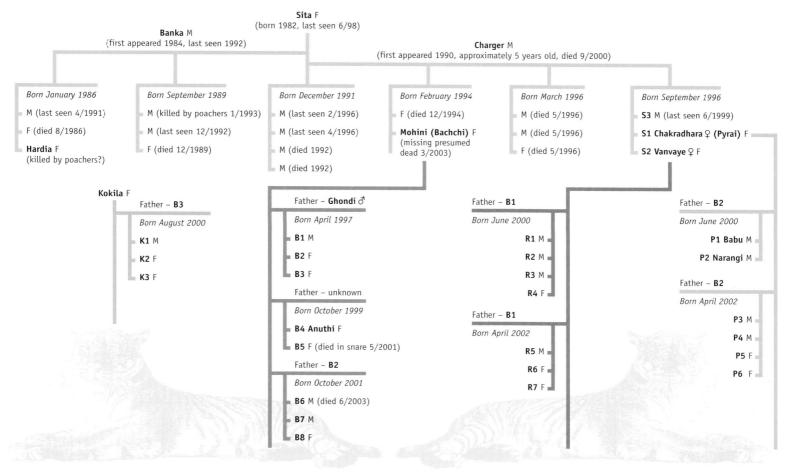

Sita F
(born 1982, last seen 6/98)

Banka M
(first appeared 1984, last seen 1992)

Charger M
(first appeared 1990, approximately 5 years old, died 9/2000)

Born January 1986
- M (last seen 4/1991)
- F (died 8/1986)
- **Hardia** F
(killed by poachers?)

Born September 1989
- M (killed by poachers 1/1993)
- M (last seen 12/1992)
- F (died 12/1989)

Born December 1991
- M (last seen 2/1996)
- M (last seen 4/1996)
- M (died 1992)
- M (died 1992)

Born February 1994
- F (died 12/1994)
- **Mohini (Bachchi)** F
(missing presumed dead 3/2003)

Born March 1996
- M (died 5/1996)
- M (died 5/1996)
- F (died 5/1996)

Born September 1996
- **S3** M (last seen 6/1999)
- **S1 Chakradhara** ♀ **(Pyrai)** F
- **S2 Vanvaye** ♀ F

Kokila F

Father – **B3**

Born August 2000
- **K1** M
- **K2** F
- **K3** F

Father – **Ghondi** ♂

Born April 1997
- **B1** M
- **B2** F
- **B3** F

Father – unknown

Born October 1999
- **B4 Anuthi** F
- **B5** F (died in snare 5/2001)

Father – **B2**

Born October 2001
- **B6** M (died 6/2003)
- **B7** M
- **B8** F

Father – **B1**

Born June 2000
- **R1** M
- **R2** M
- **R3** M
- **R4** F

Father – **B1**

Born April 2002
- **R5** M
- **R6** F
- **R7** F

Father – **B2**

Born June 2000
- **P1 Babu** M
- **P2 Narangi** M

Father – **B2**

Born April 2002
- **P3** M
- **P4** M
- **P5** F
- **P6** F

two males mating with one tigress. He says they appeared to be taking it in turns, one watching nearby while the other mated. He even suspected there was a fourth tiger in the equation, although he could not get a fix on it. He guessed that the two males were either brothers or father and son but admitted that he had never before seen such behaviour. Unfortunately, because no research is being done on Kanha's tigers, we don't know the identity of those two tolerant tigers – nor what relationship they had, if any, to their chosen female. What a pity.

A young tiger was killed in a fight in the Mukki range of Kanha in December 2002 but even this story turned out to have a twist in its tail. When there are so few left, the death of any tiger is a matter of interest, but if you want to solve a murder you need to know as much as possible about the victim. I had seen this

youngster in November. He was nearly two years old and already very big, the largest of three brothers. Two veteran Kanha observers had noticed something unusual about him. He was extremely confident and rather bossy, apparently treating his brothers as apprentices. Raj Singh had observed the way he seemed to take the lead and that he would frequently call the others to follow him as they moved through the forest. Tarun Bhati watched him try to 'organize' a chital hunt in a steep-sided dry river bed. The deer were down in the ravine and the two smaller brothers stayed at the rim, while it was the big one that plunged over the edge. Chital exploded out in all directions and the brothers jabbed idiotically at the first flying deer with their paws. Then they seemed to realize what was required of them and gave chase to a large buck. Just as they seemed to be gaining, it

sprang across another streambed. The two brothers followed suit but they didn't make it. They both fell in.

At first I thought it was surprising for a tiger like big brother to be killed. He was much too large for a male to tackle just to get at the mother. Even a 12-month-old cub can give an attacker a disabling scratch and the likelihood of 'infanticide' occurring diminishes as the cubs grow older. At the same time he was too young and insignificant to incur such savage wrath from a resident male. A tiger of his age and inexperience would run away from a serious adult and would be unlikely to be pursued to the death. Unless, of course, he didn't run away. There were two tigresses in Mukki, his mother and probably his mother's sister, with five well-grown cubs between them. When I was there in November we hardly saw a tiger. We found occasional prints over short distances but even the elephants couldn't locate them. I believed they might all be sharing a large kill and drifting away only for an occasional drink. Two days after we left they were all discovered on a gaur. The significance of this was that the two families clearly interacted peaceably together. Big brother had probably never encountered a tiger to whom he was not related and who would not tolerate his overbearing behaviour. What seems to have happened in December is that a new male came down from the hills and the youngster, uneducated in the ways of 'wilderness tigers', greeted him with inappropriate signals of dominance.

Rather than being an indication of typical Kanha violence, big brother's death may have signified the opposite. Because the other tigers around him were family and friends, he had perhaps developed a fatal precocity that in 'wilder' conditions might never have been allowed.

The 'wilderness tiger'

If tigers in the parks are becoming less violent towards each other, they are also becoming more used to humans. In Bandhavgarh and Ranthambhore they are clearly habituated to vehicles and will stalk and even kill prey close to jeeps. In areas where they are not persecuted they move about more freely in daylight. The first two hours of the morning and the last hour before dark remain by far the best times to spot them, although I have seen tigers at all times of the day. Daytime tigers, of course, can quickly revert. When poachers hit Ranthambhore in the late 1980s and early 1990s it became almost impossible to see tigers: partly because tiger numbers plummeted, but also because those that remained quickly relearned the art of invisibility.

As we know, a century ago there were possibly 100,000 tigers in the world. Their habitat was largely continuous, covering huge expanses of forest right across Asia. The opportunities for dispersal must have been almost infinite and the isolated little genetic islands that we have today did not exist. Instead, the world must have had a 'wilderness tiger' – an animal that might reasonably hope never to encounter a human; an animal with

Left: Charger, the famous old male of Bandhavgarh.
Above right: Tigers will even use jeeps to hide behind when they are stalking.

dense jungle and vast spaces in which to disappear; an animal that would never be constrained to live cheek-by-jowl with its own relatives. The tragedy is that we know so very little about that animal.

Ethology, the study of animal behaviour from the animal's point of view, did not really establish itself as a discipline until the 1950s. The work of Nobel laureates Niko Tinbergen and Konrad Lorenz marked a watershed in natural history. After them came works like Bryan Nelson's seminal studies of seabirds, in which he tries to interpret the posturing of gannets and auks by what they mean to the birds rather than by what they look like to the human eye. Before them there were travellers' tales, anthropomorphic observations which often told you as much about the writer as they did about the animal. Here are two passages for comparison:

It was deeply frustrating to watch a gannet with its egg or small chick slightly displaced. The simplest thing in the world would seem to be for the adult to pick it up gently in that most precise and skilful implement, the bill, and put it where it should be. If the out-of-place object is a scrap of nest material no effort is too great. The gannet will try again and again, with unfathomable patience, to pick it up with the tips of the mandibles, so delicately that if it were a goldcrest's egg it wouldn't break. But its own egg or chick does not register as 'nest material' (why should it?) and does not trigger picking-up behaviour. The gannet does not, and presumably cannot 'think' about it, and use its skills in a novel context.

And:

The tigress had seen me, or she would not have crossed the pool and hurried for shelter, as her tracks showed she had

done. Having seen me she had also seen that I was alone, and watching me from cover as she undoubtedly was, she would assume I was going to the pool to drink as she had done. My movements up to this had been quite natural, and if I could continue to make her think I was unaware of her presence, she would possibly give me a second chance.

The first extract is from Bryan Nelson's *Living with Seabirds*, published in 1986, but based on studies begun in 1960. The second dates from 1946 and comes from Jim Corbett's *Man-eaters of Kumaon*. In Nelson's work the gannets behave like birds; in Corbett's the tiger thinks like a human. Jim Corbett was a dedicated lover of nature with vast experience in the field. But he was a man of his time. Like most pre-war tiger enthusiasts, he learnt about tigers by hunting them down and shooting them. He was an expert in tracking them and knew all about how they killed their prey. Few of his subjects, however, lasted long enough in his company to teach him much about the intricacies of their family life. The whole fascinating area of the tiger's more intimate social interactions, and the behaviour of individuals towards their friends and relations as well as their enemies, was left almost

untouched. Furthermore, Corbett and his colleagues did not have the scientific tools, radio-collars and the like that we have today, or the training in objectivity that ethology has brought to the subject. Even had they wanted to be more analytical, that would have been difficult. In those days natural history was a field for the amateur, and the readership was a popular one that liked its myths to be familiar. Corbett was not only one of the best of these amateurs but also told some of the best stories:

> The track of the tigress was clearly visible. On one side of it were great splashes of blood where the girl's head had hung down, and on the other side the trail of her feet. Half a mile up the hill I found the girl's sari, and on the brow of the hill her skirt. Once again the tigress was carrying a naked woman, but mercifully on this occasion her burden was dead.

Sadly for us, however, the 'wilderness tiger' has disappeared almost without trace. Now that tigers are confined to all those little fragments of isolated vegetation, separated from each other across a vast continent, we cannot easily compare their behaviour with the past. Has isolation resulted in a more tolerant, social, less aggressive strain? I suppose we will never know. We can only register what happens from now on. One of the few things we do

know about those golden-age tigers was that some of them ate a lot of people. According to Corbett, the Chowgarh man-eater killed 64 humans from 27 villages between 1926 and 1930. The Champawat man-eater was said to have notched up its 436th victim by the time he dispatched it. But were these tigers exceptional, as man-eaters are today, or were humans a more regular dietary item then and the 'wilderness tiger' altogether a more lethal animal? And were those figures really correct? Was it

Opposite: In India's most visited parks tigers have become very relaxed.
Above: They now even hunt during the day.

certain that all those deaths were indeed the victims of tiger attacks? What a good way to cover up the removal of an unwanted family member, to say that a tiger took her, as some villagers today in Assam say a person has drowned. Then again, as in the game of conkers, the score of a man-eater passes in some secret transfer of magic to the hunter who kills it. Who could resist a little exaggeration?

Whatever the case, there is evidence to suggest that tigers confined within small forests surrounded by inhospitable farmland are becoming more tolerant towards each other and the reason may be the high level of kinship that exists between them. Whether this friendliness extends to humans is another question.

Why are so few tigers man-eaters?

When is a human most likely to be attacked?

**Does displacement make a tiger more likely
to kill humans?**

What other factors can turn tigers into man-eaters?

Why are the Sundarbans tigers so dangerous?

Is man-eating becoming more or less frequent?

Man on the Menu

Fact Over Fiction

One evening in late October 1997 I was driving through the forest at Kishanpur with my filming assistant Druv Singh. Far up the track ahead, in the last glimmer of fading light, something moved – a shadow gliding from the pale sand into the black trees. Was it a big macaque? A leopard? A tiger? When we reached the spot there was nothing. Silence and darkness. I thought it might have been a monkey, Druv was sure it was a tiger, so I decided to try calling it out. I sucked on my hand, producing a long, high-pitched squeal. It does sometimes work. At home I've often called inquisitive foxes right up to my feet in this way. At first, nothing happened. Then Druv, with his cat's eyes, said 'it's coming' and a moment later a tiger stepped out onto the path 60 m (195 feet) away, glared balefully at us and slipped back among the shadows.

We had been filming all day for *Land of the Tiger* but suddenly all fatigue was gone. We sat there in our tiny jeep, with no roof and no doors, calling into the night until there it was again, not 6 m (20 feet) away: long, lean, intense. Was it stalking us? Was it hungry? Was it just curious, like us?

Again it vanished; again I called. Then silence, as if all sound, all life, had emptied out of the forest. Minutes passed. Then I felt a faint, impossible warmth along my bare arm and, sliding my eyes to the left I filled my entire vision – my whole world – with tiger. Noiselessly, on cushioned feet, he had emerged to stand right beside me.

With one paw he could have plucked me out of my tin like an olive on a cocktail stick. So why didn't he eat me? A few years earlier I had made a BBC film about what turns a tiger into a man-eater. Injury, old age, displacement from the home range or merely an unpredictable moment of opportunism – these are all possible explanations that we will look at in due course. But what I had found most interesting was the opposite question: why, in fact, are so few tigers man-eaters? Tigers can and do kill almost anything they meet in the jungle. I have seen them attack a full-grown elephant, tackle a 7.6-m (25-foot) python, kill a young rhinoceros. So why are fewer than three in a 100 ever likely to kill a human being?

There is an amusing and apposite notice visible as you leave Bandhavgarh. It shows a huge, placid tiger and reads: 'You may not have seen me, but I have seen you.' As we know, there are now more than a billion people in India and Indian tigers probably see humans – most of them easy meat – every single day of their lives. Surely, then, it is a little strange that attacks on people are not more frequent.

It may be that they were in the past. Those huge tallies that Jim Corbett records for some of the tigers he killed imply that village life in northern India in the early twentieth century involved a state of constant siege, with man-eaters round every corner. But Corbett was responsible for dealing with them; that's what he was writing about, so his testimony may be somewhat skewed. Tigers were also 20 times more numerous in those days, so more attacks would not necessarily mean more man-eaters.

It must also be said that there is one place where tigers have gained a particularly fearsome reputation. That is in the Sundarbans, a mangrove forest on the Bay of Bengal, straddling the Indian and Bangladeshi border. The plight of its local fishermen and honey collectors has perhaps been a little hyped by numerous television documentaries but it seems to be true that more humans are eaten here than elsewhere. More of that, and of Jim Corbett, later. Suffice it to say that throughout the rest of its range the tiger generally keeps us off its menu.

It is widely assumed that the main constraint is fear but what exactly are tigers afraid of? Can they really know that we may be even better armed than they are? Surely not. And anyway, most of us aren't. Are tigers actually aware that if they kill just one of us they will bring a whole posse down on their heads? They will, but I doubt they reason that out for themselves. Do they find our smell unappetizing? Has the species programmed into its genes the bad experiences of all previous tigers with humans, so that these can be inherited as an instinctive message to avoid us? Perhaps. But I think the explanation may be more simple and, in a way, more intriguing.

As we have seen, the principle of ethology requires us to try thinking like the animal we study rather than assume that it thinks like us. We must learn to observe every tiny detail of its behaviour without imposing our own human set of significances upon its actions. The process may be a little like that of the artist who trains himself out of the literal interpretation of what he sees. He may concentrate, for instance, not on the obvious figure in the chair with the lamp behind but on the spaces between the objects – spaces defined not by words in the brain but by colours and shades of light that strike the eyes alone.

Briefly, then, I would like to pretend to 'think' like a tiger because I suspect that a tiger's fear of humans lies not in some pre-programmed ancestral logic but in the way it actually perceives us at the unique moment of contact. In other words, the tiger is frightened not by the thought of us but by what it actually sees when it meets us. To a tiger, a human in a jeep is probably just a jeep and because tigers don't eat jeeps the human is safe – unless the jeep is menacing the tiger or its cubs, in which case a brave or enraged tiger may charge. A human on foot, however, is a different sort of puzzle.

I am 1.8 m (6 feet) tall. A tiger is only 0.9 m (3 feet) tall but he is 2.7 m (9 feet) long. So when a tiger sees me, it might not be unreasonable for it to assume that I am 5.5 m (18 feet) long: not just an ugly brute but an enormous ugly brute. If it is still up for the fight, the tiger is about to encounter another obstacle. If I were an enormous deer, it would leap on my back, but when it thinks of doing this it discovers that I have no back. From the front I am huge but from the side I all but disappear. This must be very disconcerting. A hunter has to be confident it can tackle its prey before it attacks and no one is confident when disconcerted. This is especially true of a solitary hunter like the tiger. Lions, incidentally (especially young lionesses), are probably more dangerous than tigers because they tend to egg each other into taking risks. I have certainly had many more frightening run-ins with lionesses than with tigers.

If my theory is correct – that a tiger is disconcerted to find that a standing human is both very big and yet somehow invisible – then the opposite should be true of a squatting human. I have to admit that the one time I am nervous in the jungle is when I have to answer a heavy-duty call of nature in the dark and I prefer

Above: Procession with a man-eating tiger killed in Corbett National Park.
Overleaf: A Bengal tiger at its prime (six years old) patrolling its territory in winter.

to squat with my back to a tree. A couple of days before we called the tiger to us, I was spending my days in a hide in the swamp at Kishanpur and had to deal with such matters long before sunrise. On that particular morning – it was actually a few hours before the tigress attacked the python – I shone my torch up and down the little path through the forest to check there were no tigers and no fresh prints and then crept a few paces into the bushes. It was pitch black and very quiet. When you have been in the field for a while you develop a sixth sense – a feeling that something is going to happen before it does and an ability to know what is around you without seeing or hearing it. I squatted in the darkness with blithe confidence that I was safe and alone. A few minutes later I stepped back onto the path and there in the torchlight was a line of brand-new tracks. The tigress – clearly in the mood for a fight, since she was on her way to beat up the

python – had passed within swiping distance and I had not had the slightest inkling of her presence. So much for sixth sense.

A squatting human being is half the size of a standing one and presents twice the spread of back. In fact, he or she most closely resembles a medium-sized deer. If tigers were simply frightened of all humans, then a squatting person would be no more a target than a standing one. This, however, appears not to be the case. Time and time again, villagers who have been attacked have been squatting or bending over to cut grass for fodder or building material.

For myself, I can honestly say that, so far, the only time I have come perilously close to being killed by a big cat was when I was squatting down. I was filming the Gir lion sequence in Gujarat for *Land of the Tiger* and was crouching at the camera to achieve an appealingly low angle. About 36 m (120 feet) in front of me, two full-grown lion cubs were squabbling and I had asked my guard – armed with the customary stick – to sit well away from me so that they were not disturbed. We both took our eyes off the lioness, an elderly animal so ugly and scarred that I had decided not to film her. Filming is totally absorbing but suddenly, after some 20 minutes, I had what I can only describe as a horrible sense of terror. I jumped round and there crouched behind me, coiled and about to spring, was the hideous mother lion. When a big cat is going to attack its expression changes. It doesn't snarl or lay back its ears. It does the opposite. It closes its mouth, points its ears slightly forward and focuses its eyes straight through the victim. In that split second I recognized the focus. So did my guard. We both charged straight at the lioness and she seemed to check in mid-spring and whipped away. It turned out that she had killed a 12-year-old boy the previous year. He had been given permission to get out of the jeep to relieve himself.

Left: Tiger footprints in the Sundarbans where tigers still kill humans every year.

Possible causes of man-eating

More has been written about man-eating than almost any other aspect of tiger behaviour, so it is odd that this question of why it doesn't happen more often has not been more frequently investigated. Whatever the reason, man-eating does seem to be rare and it usually requires a particular set of circumstances for a tiger to overcome its natural fear or repugnance. As I have said, when I made my own film *Man-Eater: To Be or Not To Be* with Richard Brock in 1992, I based it on a case study by David Smith. Among the tigers he had been studying in Chitwan National Park in Nepal was one that he called Bahadur Bhale, born on Banderjola island near the edge of the park in May 1980. In March 1984 Smith was canoeing along the Rapti river when he witnessed a fierce fight between Bahadur Bhale and the local dominant male, Bangi Bhale. We have already seen that this may have been partly provoked by Bahadur Bhale's 'illicit' interest in female 122, whose young cubs had vanished three months earlier (she was actually to be Bahadur's last mate, producing three cubs in July 1987), but the flashpoint seems to have been a disputed kill. What was interesting was what happened next. Bangi Bhale, though he was older and the incumbent male, lost the fight. He fled into the river limping badly. Injured and displaced from his customary haunts, he began to hang around the park perimeter. In May he killed a man cutting grass and two buffaloes. In June he killed another man and in August he killed a woman.

In India and Nepal a tiger that kills a human is not necessarily treated as a man-eater. If the tragedy is believed to be the result of an unfortunate accidental encounter, the tiger will be spared, though its subsequent movements will, where possible, be carefully monitored. Only if there is clear evidence of intention – signs, for instance, that the tiger has stalked its victims or returned to look for the body – will the animal be removed. In December 1984 Bangi attacked again and he was then darted and removed to Kathmandu Zoo, where he died in sad confinement six years later.

But this was only the beginning of the story. In September 1985 'my' tiger, Bahadur Bhale, fought a second, much more dominant male tiger called Kancha Bhale. This quarrel definitely coincided with the first oestrus cycle of a young female in Kancha's range called K. P., with which Bahadur Bhale was eventually to have two cubs in May 1987. The two males fought again in October and November and on 9 January 1986, when Kancha too was injured and abandoned the area to the all-powerful Bahadur. And what did Kancha do? He headed for the villages on the edge of the park where, within three weeks he killed nine cattle and buffaloes and a man. He was shot dead in March a few hours after killing his fourth victim.

Kancha himself had displaced another male, 127, which, as he was forced westwards away from his own original range, had also taken to killing people. Between October 1980 and April 1981 he was believed to have eaten five humans. Two of the killings were apparently committed in the company of a female tiger, 118, and all of them in habitat that was rich in natural prey. According to Charles McDougal, however, 127 then established a new home range containing two tigresses and, even though the following January (1982) thousands of grass-cutters entered his area for their annual two-week harvest, he never killed again.

Between 1964 and 1979 there had been no known cases of man-eating in Chitwan. For nearly half this period the main study area had enjoyed a span of unusual stability in which one or two males held constant sway over a large range. We have already seen that this resulted in extraordinarily high productivity, reminding us how crucial competent males actually are to the breeding success of the species. For the same reasons it would appear that stability among males is also a very important factor in minimizing cases of man-eating. Conversely, 13 people were killed in Chitwan in the early 1980s and this coincided with a great deal of conflict between competing males. It was also a disastrous period for reproduction, with no cubs surviving to

dispersal in an area that had been an absolute kindergarten in the mid- to late 1970s. Once Bahadur Bhale settled in, however – enjoying the company of no fewer than seven females – productivity recovered and there were no further instances of man-eating.

The reason why conflict can lead to man-eating is not merely because tigers get injured and displaced, lose their familiar hunting grounds and are forced to resort to desperate measures. There is an essential additional factor. These displaced tigers are adults, former range-holders, dominant animals. They can be especially dangerous when in trouble because they are confident characters. Young tigers start their adult lives in a state of displacement but are less likely to have the courage to tackle humans. Older tigers are a different matter. I believe this fundamental aspect of tiger biology was neglected by the hunters of old. They did not take into account the imbalances that their own actions might cause in a tiger population. They liked to hunt trophy males. Every big tiger they killed was likely to be a dominant range-holder and his death would leave a gap that others would fight to fill. The result: constant instability. It may

well be that the very act of hunting was creating man-eating situations and that the brave protectors of the villagers, like Jim Corbett, were actually exacerbating the situation and that this partly explains why man-eating seems to have been more common in the past. How much more we learn from studying tigers rather than shooting them.

Not all of Chitwan's man-eaters, however, were displaced males. There were several incidences of tigresses attacking humans in Chitwan in the early 1980s. One case was a mystery. According to David Smith, a tigress called BP2 killed three people in a year and then never killed again. She was monitored for at least two subsequent years but kept a clean slate. Other examples were more conventional. A tigress called Bungi Poti was injured by her daughter and pushed out of her range. She was then mauled by a male when she came to the bait at Tiger Tops and ended slipping ignominiously on the newly washed dung floor in a village hut where she had attacked somebody. Another tigress, Mari, apparently took livestock from inside a house. The owners chased her into a field and threw stones at her but two people who ventured too close were severely mauled. The next day Mari walked into yet another house at dinnertime. The owners ran out the back door and she was subsequently darted and put to death. She was found to be old, in poor health and with very bad teeth.

In 1987 Charles McDougal wrote an excellent chapter on man-eating for the book *Tigers of the World*, in which he summarized the relative frequency of attacks on humans in different parts of the tiger's range. Records had been carefully collected by numerous historians and naturalists, such as R. G. Burton, A. Locke and Richard Perry, and they showed that in almost all the countries where tigers were found – specifically Myanmar (Burma), Thailand, Vietnam, Malaysia, Sumatra, Java and the Caspian region – man-eating was extremely rare. There were two intriguing exceptions. In Myanmar Perry reported a local outbreak in the Arakan region during the Second World War.

It seems that tigers learnt to scavenge corpses left during the great retreat of 1942 and later started to kill people. In Vietnam the same thing happened during the Vietnam War. In the USSR the biologist V. Abramov recorded no instances of man-eating between 1917 and 1962. There have only been a couple since. A tiger was shot on the streets of Vladivostok in March 1986 but it had lived on dogs for six months and on the whole the Siberian tiger, with its huge, sparsely populated territory, has not developed a taste for humans.

This leaves just three areas where tigers have had a strong inclination for human meat. The first is south China: 60 people were reported killed in a single village in Fukien province in 1922. But by that time most of the natural habitat had been destroyed, there was little wild prey left and the tigers themselves have since become all but extinct. The second problem area was Singapore. Burton recorded that tigers that had crossed onto the once wild and swampy island from the Malay mainland were hard-pressed for habitat by the 1840s and that 200–300 people were being killed there each year, while the death-toll on the other islands was even higher. Pit-traps and hunters had more or less wiped out the tigers by 1949 but 20 years earlier the death-rate was still 15 people a year. In both these cases, lack of alternative food seems to have been the main reason for turning on man.

The third human killing field was India, where even as late as the 1930s, 1000 people a year were reported as being eaten by tigers. On average, half of these attacks occurred in Bengal, which included the dreaded Sundarbans mangrove swamps. This area is associated with a uniquely vicious strain of tiger but it is clear that the Sundarbans population is only a relic of the tigers that were cleaned out elsewhere by agriculture. It may be that all

Left: An injured tiger may sometimes become a man-eater.
Above right: Charging tiger. If a tiger was going to kill you, you might not see it as it would probably come from behind.

the tigers of the region were bloodthirsty or that much of the initial conflict was due to loss of habitat and the destruction of natural prey. That was a conflict the tiger was bound to lose, in which case man-eating was a last-ditch activity rather than standard behaviour. There seem to have been two other flashpoints for conflict. One was the central provinces, mainly Madhya Pradesh. This remains the core of India's tiger population and McDougal concludes that man-eating was rife mainly in the areas that were being opened up by railways and roads. Finally, there were the famous man-eaters of the united provinces, the northern hills bordering Nepal where Corbett made his name. Again according to McDougal, these tigers (both male and

female) seem to have been pushed into marginal habitats by saturated tiger populations in the last natural lowlands. It is thought they followed domestic livestock that wintered in the plains and moved to summer pastures in the hills. As McDougal says, such 'tigers were the old, the young and the disabled. Of 16 notorious man-eaters of the period, 10 were females. All suffered from some disability, mainly caused by gunshot wounds or porcupine quills... these tigers probably only attacked porcupines when other prey was scarce or difficult to hunt.'

The generation of men who could have witnessed the depredations of tigers has passed away. We are left with mere statistics. These – as we are well aware – can be manipulated and exaggerated. How meticulously were they collected in the first place? Was every incident properly investigated? Is it possible

that some of the tigers' victims were knocked off by their neighbours or lost to some accident? If so, how many? Did the notorious Talla Des and Lohaghat Tigresses really notch up a tally of 150 people each between the wars, as Corbett and J. Hewett attest, or might there have been just a little bit of hearsay involved in the accounting process? One day all these figures will have to be checked but that's a job for the dedicated local historian. In the meantime, there is one place where, even today, tigers seem to exhibit a motiveless malignancy towards human beings.

Above: A large resident male in Nepal. When tigers are displaced from their home range they can become man-eaters.

The Sundarbans killing fields

The Sundarbans is said to be the world's largest delta. It is formed by the Ganges, Brahmaputra and Meghana rivers where they mingle to flow into the Bay of Bengal south of Calcutta. The vast pattern of channels, sandflats, islands and mangrove forests spreads over 10,000 sq km (3860 square miles). Roughly 40 per cent of it lies within India and the rest belongs to Bangladesh. It contains an unknown number of tigers, said to be around 300, and for some reason they have always eaten a lot of humans. As early as 1887 E. E. Baker described the Sundarbans tiger as being characterized by 'its utter fearlessness of man, and its inveterate propensity to kill and devour him on all and every opportunity'. Between 1983 and 1985 Mohammad Khan reported that deaths had fallen to a low of 22 per year! In his 1990 book *Tigers*, Peter Jackson described a typical incident witnessed by a fisherman called Nagar Ali in May 1969. Ali was on his boat at night cooking supper for his friend Malek Molla. He heard a splash, turned round and realized that Malek had gone. There on the river bank stood a tiger 'holding Malek Molla's body in its jaws, like a cat with a fish'. And just as a cat would with a fish, the tiger ate him. This was no accident. This was a tiger on the hunt for humans. There is no acute shortage of wild prey in the Sundarbans, which supports a good population of chital and wild boar. Nor are these regular, unprovoked attacks primarily associated with loss of habitat, extreme disturbance or displacement. It really does seem that the Sundarbans tigers like eating people.

In the first three months of 1971 a German biologist, Dr Hubert Hendrichs, studied the Sundarbans tigers in Bangladesh. He estimated that up to one-third of them were likely to attack people on sight and might well eat them, even though fewer than 1 per cent were probably mainstream man-eaters. He believed the problem might be the high salinity of the water and a subsequent study by M. K. Chowdbury and P. Sanyal in 1985 showed that although fewer people entered the Sundarbans in April and May, more of them were killed then and that was also the time when salinity in the water sources peaked. Consequently, the authorities built a number of freshwater tanks for the tigers to drink from. Sadly, the number of casualties continued unabated at an average of 47 a year but the tigers did favour the new pools and it may be that there will be a long-term benefit. In 1979 permits to areas where the palm *Phoenix paludosa* grows were withdrawn. The tigers there often make their dens in palm thickets, so it was hoped that this measure would reduce disturbance and the risk of face-to-face encounters; over the next four years the average annual death-toll fell slightly to 43.

But Chowdbury and Sanyal came up with another fascinating statistic. The tigers of the Sundarbans were all right-handed. At least, every single fatal bite was found to be on the right-hand side of the victim's nape. This prompted some imaginative defence measures. People entering the swamps to gather wood or honey were told to carry a stout stick on their right shoulders. Some of them also began wearing a three-piece fibreglass tiger-helmet over the nape, neck and chest, with spikes set in the back. This sounds unwieldy but did deter tigers, as did the wearing of face masks with big eyes on the back of the head. Although fishermen comprised only 70 per cent of the humans entering the Sundarbans, they accounted for 82 per cent of the victims and it was not practical for them to carry sticks while they worked their boats and nets, so another more extreme device was mooted: aversion therapy. The authorities built a number of life-size human dummies out of painted clay, all suffused with human scent. There were dummy fishermen in boats, dummy woodcutters squatting on the ground and dummy honey-collectors. They were placed at strategic locations in the buffer zone of the national park, where most attacks had occurred, and were wired up to car batteries. In a report for *Tigers of the World* in 1987 Sanyal described what happened to a dummy fisherman.

The dummy had been set in December 1984, and the position and garments were periodically changed. Between 6 a.m. and 4 p.m., the energizer for the model was routinely switched off. In February 1985, the tiger pounced on the model at 8 a.m., tore the dummy into pieces, roared and kept the torso by its side for three hours in view of the assigned group of staff.

In all, a total of 11 dummies were attacked between June 1983 and January 1986 and, where a tiger had received an electric shock, the aversion therapy seemed to have been effective. These measures together had, since 1983, halved the number of attacks to an annual average of 22. One snag was keeping the batteries charged. Solar panels were tried, though with limited success. It has also proved time-consuming to maintain the dummies and check on them regularly. Perhaps the most interesting aspect of the experiment was that it worked at all. The fact that the tigers would actually attack dummy human beings indicates an extraordinarily robust attitude among the Sundarbans tigers. In which case there is an intriguing fact tucked away in the statistics collected when man-eating in India was at its peak. Burton claimed that 455 people were killed by tigers in Bengal in 1908. Yet in 1910 Sainthill Eardley-Wilmot said that the average death-toll in the Sundarbans was 60–70 – a mere 15 per cent of the total that Burton suggests for the province. In other words, it looks as if the tigers of that whole region took an unwholesome interest in humans and that the Sundarbans tigers may be just a relic of a larger, very bloodthirsty clan.

Between 1980 and 1985 the honey harvest in the Sundarbans National Park increased by 90 per cent, a sign not only that depredation by tigers had decreased but that local people had realized the benefits accruing from a better knowledge of tigers. The provision of fresh water, the use of protective clothing and sticks, and the electrified dummies not only helped to divert tigers from humans but also persuaded local people that the authorities were taking an interest in their problems, thereby providing a good model for other communities.

Although the Sundarbans tigers do appear to be exceptional, it would be wrong to exaggerate their devilishness. The main reason why attacks are so frequent is because so many people enter the swamps, then stay for long periods, often bent double and absorbed in their work, and often in deep cover where tigers may approach them without warning. To put this into perspective, it is worth remembering that even four years of 'pugmark' studies in the 1980s led to the conclusion that no more than 5 per cent of the tigers there might be true man-eaters and this was probably an upper estimate. There is another interesting statistic that affects the Sundarbans: it has, comparatively recently, lost more of its natural prey species than almost any other tiger habitat. Local extinctions include hog deer, barasingha, Indian and Javan rhino and buffalo.

On the whole, tigers eat people because they have been interfered with in some way – disturbed, injured or displaced. In areas where there are large numbers of tigers, and people creep around their habitat without giving them due warning, attacks will be more frequent. I suspect that if every tourist who visited Bandhavgarh was expected to crawl through the bushes on all-fours, a lot would get eaten. I would be chary of visiting the park myself under such conditions! In fact, a tragedy occurred there on 29 March 2003, which illustrates a likely cause of attacks. Seven jeeps were stopped at 'Charger Point' listening to chital alarm calls when a tigress appeared. She was bleeding at the mouth and suddenly ran at the rearmost vehicle; she made as if to swerve around it and then – to everyone's absolute astonishment – she leapt into the back. Two French tourists flattened themselves beneath her and eventually a local guide came to their rescue. The tigress bit the guide and then wandered off. The mystery was that, although the attack lasted several minutes, no one was

seriously hurt. It eventually emerged that the tigress had lost three of her four canines and probably had a broken jaw – the result, it is now thought, of an accidental collision with a car on the nearby public road. The tigress seems to have been Charger's famous daughter Mohini (Bachchi). She hasn't been seen since and left three 18-month-old cubs to fend for themselves – one has subsequently died of blood poisoning from a porcupine injury.

In his man-eating chapter in *Tigers of the World* McDougal made a worrying prediction: 'As the existing habitat outside parks and reserves, where tigers are multiplying, becomes progressively fragmented and degraded owing to ever greater human encroachment, we may expect an increased incidence of problem tigers.'

In August 2002 the state government of Kelantan in Malaysia announced its intention to use the army to kill all the tigers in Tanah Merah and Jeli districts after several people had been attacked there. Fortunately, this threat was not carried out and, so far, man-eating incidents do not appear to have increased elsewhere. Provided the tiger-range nations manage their reserves and buffer zones carefully, there is no reason for conflict to escalate. Indeed, it must not. For history shows that where tigers make too bold and determined a play for resources wanted by humans they lose everything. If McDougal's prediction ever comes true, it will mean the end for the tiger.

Above: Fishermen in the Sundarbans wearing face masks on the backs of their heads to deter tigers.

Counting Tigers
What Threats Do They Face?

Outside the main entrance to the headquarters of Kaziranga National Park there is a large green noticeboard. On it are painted quaint little representations of the different mammals in the park with figures next to them something like this: rhinoceros 1261, elephant 345, tiger 56, sloth bear 22, pangolin 12, python 3. The figures have a sort of mythic power. In truth no one has the faintest idea how many pangolins or pythons there are in the park but every year the animals in all of India's major forest reserves are supposed to be censused. The usual system for counting tigers is the 'pugmark' method. Dozens of forest staff and volunteers are let loose in every park, each armed with a small glass frame on four little legs and a large wodge of tracing paper.

When someone finds a clear set of fresh tiger tracks, they place the glass over them and trace the pattern of the toes and pads onto the glass, selecting examples of all four paws if possible. They then trace from the glass onto the tracing paper, noting the date, time, soil type and precise location before cleaning off the glass for the next tracing. The papers are all collated by a senior official, who has to work out from the designs and the extraneous information which sets of prints belong to different tigers.

The system has some elemental value in that any record of fresh prints is a reassuring indication of the presence of tigers and the process involves the foresters in their welfare. But as a precise science it has some problems. It derives from the era when hunters were accompanied by 'shikaris', experienced trackers who believed they could distinguish every individual tiger from its marks. Some of them probably could. Charles McDougal worked with some very skilful Nepalis in Chitwan whose accuracy was proved in the 1970s and early 1980s when 'their' tigers were radio-collared by the Smithsonian scientists. But such field craft has to be honed by years of practice which the demise of hunting has put a stop to. Three days of census work a year

does not make anyone into a 'shikari'. The broad pugs of a male can usually be distinguished from the narrower prints and more pointed toes of a female – and some idiosyncrasies, like damaged toes, will be visible to a careful observer. But such features (especially relative size) can be masked or can vary in different types of soil (soft sand, hard mud, gravel) and most trackers who glance at a print and tell you which tiger it belongs to are probably bluffing. The other problem with the census is a political one. Field directors inherit the numbers of animals in their park as a sort of state-owned asset. Only the most courageous officer is going to admit that he has 'lost' some of the park's capital, so there has been a tendency for census numbers to admit a little annual inflation or at least be held stable.

In an experiment conducted in the early 1990s Ullas Karanth decided to put the pugmark method to test. He traced a selection of prints left by just four individual tigers inhabiting an enclosure. He then sent the results to six wildlife managers who were asked to use their normal collating methods to estimate the number and sexes of the tigers involved. Their ability to separate forepaws from hind paws and male from female was reasonably accurate. This proved that they were not idiots. Not one of them, however, managed to identify any of the individual tigers consistently and their estimates of the total population of tigers involved were wild. One respondent said there were 24 tigers, another said 6, one said 23, another 13, one said, 'don't know' and the last said 7. I'm glad I wasn't tested. I would certainly have got them wrong.

While the pugmark method continues to be used by the Indian Forest Department as a basic census device, scientists have more accurate counting methods. One way to know how many tigers you've got is to chase after them, tranquillize them all and attach radio-collars to them. But this takes a lot of work, is frankly risky to the tigers since pumping a large animal full of chemicals can kill it and is only justifiable if a great deal of other

intimate behavioural information is going to be gathered. As a way of counting tigers it's over the top. The most effective method is to use camera traps. Usually a pair of stills cameras, armed with flash, are placed either side of a likely tiger trail. The trail is crossed by an infrared beam set at tiger height which fires the cameras when it is broken. The cameras can be rigged to fire, for instance, only once in a given minute so that an entire roll of film is not expended on a jolly herd of wild pigs. Every single tiger has a unique pattern of stripes so careful scrutiny of the photographs the tigers take of themselves will allow the scientists to identify them. It is unlikely that all the tigers in a given area will be caught on film. Instead, the scientists note the number of

times the same tigers are re-photographed. They can then apply a standard sampling formula based on the proportion of new tigers to 'recaptures' to estimate the actual tiger population.

Camera-trapping is expensive and time-consuming. Reasonably reliable shortcuts can be taken by concentrating effort on a confined but representative area of a park. If a typical 100-sq-km (38½-square-mile) block, for instance, is found to hold four resident tigers, then it may be fair to conclude that the park has a density of one tiger per 25 sq km (9½ square miles) and a total population of the park's total area divided by 25 (9½). So a 1000-sq-km (386-square-mile) park would be estimated to have 40 tigers.

Another method – having of course first checked that you do actually have some tigers – is to count the prey available. Since a tiger needs 500 deer to support the 50 or so deer it munches through each year then an area with, say, 4000 deer or equivalent weight of prey can, in principle, support eight tigers. Conversely,

Opposite: Tigers are censused in India, often inaccurately.
Above: Counting prey is a guide to the carrying capacity of a tiger's habitat – no prey, no tigers.

Top: Camera traps are set on trails so tigers can
photograph themselves.
Above: Tiger being radio-collared in Nepal.

if you only have 100 deer you can't expect to have any resident
tigers at all. To estimate prey numbers you walk along transects –
representative strips of habitat – counting the prey you see and
recording their distance from you. This gives a representative
sample population, which you then multiply by the number of
transects that comprise the total area being counted. From this
figure you can estimate the potential carrying capacity for tigers.

An even more hands–off, long-distance method is to use
satellite pictures of habitat, assume that a given habitat area will
hold the sort of tiger population that known equivalents hold and
then do a series of spot checks. This way you could look at maps
of the entire tiger range throughout Asia, make an educated
guess at how many tigers they ought to hold and then visit one in
each country and do a more accurate count. Broadly speaking,
this was David Smith's idea. He felt that tigers might not have
time to wait to be counted by more formal methods and that some
intelligent sweeping guesses might be helpful. The problem, as he
would be the first to admit, is that good–looking forests don't
always mean tigers and so far – until we know more about the
variables – remote census methods are probably only helpful in
the most peripheral way. They show us where tigers could be –
and where they cannot be – but not actually where they are.

There is one other way to count tigers which I suspect will
be used increasingly over the next decade. DNA samples
identifying individual animals can now be extracted from scats.
For the moment, this is a high-tech method which is not readily
available to everyone in the field and laboratories probably don't
want to be clogged up with tiger dung but eventually it may
become commonplace. After all, when the first tiger was radio-
collared in December 1973 that was considered an expensive and
specialized technique. Now there are radio-collared tigers in
several Indian reserves, including Panna and Nagarahole, as well
as in Siberia and, most recently, Sumatra. Furthermore, new
devices being used on wolves in Scandinavia allow scientists to
download information via satellites every half hour direct from
collar to computer without even having to see the wolves after
their initial capture and release. In the future, a scientist will
be able to plod around the tiger's habitat, downloading remote
data or scooping droppings into separate, labelled,
uncontaminated bags for analysis without ever needing to
disturb his subject.

In the meantime, however, even though the tiger is the most charismatic of the world's endangered animals, we really do not know how many are left. Every possible method has been used to estimate their numbers but tigers are thinly distributed across a vast expanse of earth, much of it environmentally or politically inhospitable to scientists. In India alone there are reckoned to be over 300,000 sq km (115,800 square miles) of probable tiger habitat. It has not yet proved practical to search even this area properly. In the meantime, an article published in Spring 2003 by Ullas Karanth, John Seidensticker, Charles McDougal and others in the London-based journal *Animal Conservation* argued that 30 years of tiger conservation in India have been predicated on completely inaccurate survey methods – namely the pugmark system.

How many and where do they live?

Tigers today inhabit 13 or perhaps 14 countries in Asia. These are India, Nepal, Bangladesh, Bhutan, Myanmar (Burma), Thailand, Indonesia, Vietnam, Cambodia, Laos, Malaysia, Russia (Siberia only), China and, occasionally, North Korea. The bulk of the population – among the best studied and probably the best protected tigers – live in India. Yet even there estimates vary widely from pessimistic conservationists who believe there may be as few as 2000 to the most recent official statistics that claimed 3646 in the 2001–2 census. So when we say, as most us do, that there are 2500–3000 tigers in India, we are only splitting the difference between two informed guesses. The Siberian region of the Russian Federation is certainly the best-researched tiger range and numbers there are put reliably at between 400 and 450. Nepal has around 100, perhaps a few more, Bhutan maybe 100 and Bangladesh probably 150.

Heading east, Myanmar's forests cover some 40 per cent of the land, especially the rugged uplands, and the government gave an estimate of 600–1000 tigers as their basis for establishing a National Tiger Action Plan in 1996. This included the laudable aim of increasing protected areas from 1 per cent to 5 per cent of the land mass, though so far only two of these are larger than 1000 sq km (386 square miles). The biggest is Htamanthi Wildlife Sanctuary but when this was surveyed by Alan Rabinowitz and his Wildlife Conservation Society (WCS) team in 1995, signs of tigers were very 'scarce'. The researchers also stumbled on local hunters setting snares for tigers inside the reserve. Between 1999 and 2002 WCS and the Myanmar Forest Department surveyed 17 key areas. Tiger numbers in these may actually be as low as from 150–230.

For many years Thailand was thought to contain the bulk of the so-called Indo-Chinese population, with a minimum of 500–600 tigers supported by a good forest infrastructure: at least 45 wildlife sanctuaries and 65 national parks, covering 68,849 sq km (26,575 square miles). Satellite data show 26 per cent forest cover, half of it in parks and reserves. However, a 1989 study by Alan Rabinowitz in Huai Kha Khaeng, one of the country's biggest reserves, found depressingly low tiger densities, prompting him to further surveys and questionnaires throughout the country and a halving of the estimated tiger population to 250 animals. In 1999 Smith, S. Tunhikorn, S. Tanhan and colleagues reported their remote census survey of 15 potential tiger habitats covering 43,356 sq km (16,735 square miles). They thought that the Huai Kha Khaeng/Thung Yai World Heritage Site, along with 12 parks and wildlife sanctuaries, could support a theoretical population of 178 tigers, making it potentially one of the five most important tiger areas in the world. Only three other sites, however, could hold more than 35 tigers and another nine were likely to support fewer than 20. This meant that even the potential viable population was only 300 and part of that was shared with neighbouring countries. Neil Challis of Wild Watch, Thailand, has since suggested to me that the population may be as low as 100–200.

Malaysia protected its tigers in 1976 and is supposed to have a strong population. In 1990 R. Topani, using reported sightings and some field surveys, estimated the population at 482–520. In 1996 the government, without significant further fieldwork increased these estimates to 600–650. Only one site (Taman Negara National Park) has actually been censused (1998–2002). Its population is put at 52–84 adult tigers. Elsewhere, recent reports, of forest workers being attacked by starving tigers and of desperate animals wandering onto main roads to be squashed by trucks, imply that widespread logging and development are putting Malaysia's tigers under severe pressure. Peninsular Malaysia has lost 30 per cent of its forests since the 1960s and since Taman Negara is probably its best tiger habitat, an overall figure even of 500 may prove optimistic.

Tiger habitat
- Current/potential habitat
- Range c.1900

The Indonesian population is in Sumatra. Neil Franklin and colleagues began a camera-trapping study in Way Kambas National Park in the southeast corner of the island in August 1995 and, despite the absence of tiger signs in the area and the fact that local villagers had never seen a tiger in recent years, a minimum of 21 individuals were identified. This gave hope that the other four main blocks of habitat in Sumatra might also hold more tigers than was initially feared. WCS conducted a recent camera-trap survey in Bukit Barisan in the southwest and found 40–50 and scientists are now a little more hopeful that the guess of 400 animals, which has done the rounds for many years, may be a trustworthy minimum.

As for the other countries, it is still mostly guesswork. Cambodia had until recently been out of bounds for so long that no one knew what was there. It is supposed to enjoy 56 per cent forest cover but in 1997 14 tigers were killed just in Virachey National Park and Cambodian poachers are said to use land mines to bump them off. A figure of 300 possible tigers is a pure guess. Illegal logging is said to be rife throughout the valuable tiger habitat along the Vietnamese border and forest cover has declined by 10 per cent in the last 40 years. Nevertheless, there is an active conservation project being conducted by WCS and the Cambodian government in Seima Biodiversity Conservation Area in the southeast and the staff there do see tigers. Vietnam has 100 'protected areas' and 11 national parks but only one is bigger than 1000 sq km (386 square miles) and with more than 200 people per sq km (526 people per square mile) it has lost more than 80 per cent of its forest cover since the 1940s. The IUCN's 1996 'Status of the Tiger' report suggested 200–300 tigers there but this was based on questionnaires from a 1993 survey, making

the figures are a decade old. A pugmark survey in the late 1990s found 20 tigers in two provinces in the south of the country, so there are tigers there. According to Joe Walston of WCS Cambodia, however, Vietnam is no longer a serious tiger range state. Laos still had 47 per cent forest cover in 1991 but clearance proceeds at a pace. It has at least 18 protected areas but in 1994 Alan Rabinowitz estimated the tiger population of one of the largest, Nakai–Nam Theun refuge, at only 20–30 animals, which he described as 'terribly low for the size and potential of the area'. Shall we say 100 tigers for Laos?

That leaves China and North Korea. Until the 1960s China had thousands of tigers – indeed, it had its very own subpopulation, the 'South China' tiger, but the appallingly ignorant Chairman Mao put paid to that. Chairman Mao didn't like wildlife and tigers were muscularly re–educated with guns and snares – almost all of them. Optimists still say there are 30 left. A 'South China' tiger was shot by a poacher in 1994 and the Chinese say there are a handful left. Who knows? A few wander in from Siberia in the north but are usually poached. Official statistics delivered to CITES (the Convention on International Trade in Endangered Species) in 2000 stated there were 20 tigers in Tibet and 30–40 along China's western Indo–Chinese border. A recent personal communication from Xishuangbanna Nature Reserve in the western province of Yunnan said tigers were beginning to be

Opposite: Map showing present (darker areas) and past
– c. 1900 – (lighter areas) ranges of the tiger.
Above: Aerial view of deforestation in Khao Pra-Bang,
Khram WS – the last lowland forest in Thailand.

seen again in the park. Even though China has 926 nature reserves, like North Korea (which may also occasionally have a few stragglers from the north) it makes no real contribution to world tiger numbers other than by failing – so far – to stop a disastrous market in tiger parts.

If we accept these figures we get a total world population of wild tigers of between 4560 at the most gloomy and 7026 at the most optimistic. For the last ten years there has been a rough consensus that even without counting them there are 5000–7000 tigers left. So far no one has been able seriously to challenge these estimates so there they stand.

It's a sad decline for an animal that once held sway across the Middle East and Asia, from the mountains of Turkey and the swamps of Iran, through continuous forest to the Pacific Ocean. By

examining hunting records between 1850 and 1940 and from our historical knowledge of the previous extent of forest cover, it is estimated that there were around 100,000 tigers in the world in 1900. There may have been more. The density in prime areas was staggering. Valmik Thapar believes there were 40,000 tigers just in India. He has reviewed the accounts of over 10,000 successful hunts from that period. He notes that the Maharaja of Surguja, alone, shot 1100 tigers and, as late as 1938–39, Lord Linlithgow, a former Viceroy of India, shot 120 tigers in Chitwan in just ten weeks.

These monumental bags, of course, go a long way to explain the tiger's demise. As guns became cheaper and increasingly

Above: Results of a tiger hunt *c.* 1904 in Hyderabad, India.
Opposite: Skins confiscated from poachers in Russia in 1995.

sophisticated and colonialism weakened its grip, more and more people went out to kill tigers. Furthermore, the removal of a threat meant that the forests were safer for livestock and farmers and the fading tigers lost their hold on a fast–changing landscape.

First steps in conservation

India was the first country to protect tigers by law but this did not happen until 1970, when the Prime Minister, Indira Gandhi, a vigorous conservationist, pushed through legislation to outlaw tiger hunting and the sale of tiger skins. Two years later the Indian Government organized some 5000 forest officers to complete the first nationwide tiger census. The result was shocking. The estimate came to just 1827 animals.

By then, the IUCN (International Union for the Conservation of Nature and Natural Resources) had woken up to the tiger's plight. In 1969 the tiger was given Red Data Book status, an official listing as an endangered species. Guy Mountfort, a revered British conservationist, pushed for the establishment of 'Operation Tiger', an IUCN/WWF (World Wide Fund for Nature) initiative to raise funds to conserve tigers where he thought they had the best chance of surviving, in the Indian subcontinent. The governments of India, Nepal, Bangladesh and Bhutan all declared their commitment to the project and the subsequent international appeal raised £800,000 ($1.2 million) in 18 months. Indira Gandhi set up a special tiger co-ordinating committee, under the chairmanship of an influential and aristocratic figure, Dr Karan Singh. The committee earmarked

Above: A trophy from a tiger hunt in 1972 (middle) and
claws, paws and bones from tigers poached in the 1990s.

nine areas as special tiger reserves and budgeted £2.1 million ($3.1 million) to cover the first five-year plan. Expenditure by the Indian Government has, ever since, far outstripped that by any other international body.

In July 1973 India's 'Project Tiger' was finally launched with a ceremony on the banks of the Ramganga River. This occurred in the beautiful National Park named after Jim Corbett in the state where he had lived, hunted and latterly tried to protect tigers, Uttar Pradesh, and the project's first director was Kailash Sankhala. These people all belong in the tiger's Hall of Fame. For without them and the political will that they concentrated upon the project, the tiger's demise would not have been arrested.

There are now 27 Project Tiger reserves in India and while that initial political enthusiasm amongst the high officers of state has faded, the fact that the project has become an accepted institution has ensured a basic continuity of effort within the subcontinent. For a while, however, the international community and the WWF, believing they had saved the tiger, turned their attention elsewhere and a certain complacency set in. In 1984 respected tiger researcher H. S. Panwar wrote an article for a Smithsonian book edited by McNeely and Miller called *National Parks, Conservation and Development* entitled 'What To Do When You've Succeeded: Project Tiger, Ten Years Later'. What he did not see, because no one was looking for it, was that a freight train was about to smash head-on into the project.

The new tiger crisis

One of the first people to perceive the looming disaster was Valmik Thapar. He was writing evocative accounts of the tigers of Ranthambhore and when these individuals – Genghis and Noon and the others – were beautifully filmed by Stanley Breedon and Belinda Wright, they became familiar to an international audience. But then Genghis disappeared. Then Noon. At first Thapar assumed they had died of natural causes but by the late 1980s tigers were becoming invisible at Ranthambhore. Official census figures still maintained that there were about 40 tigers there but neither Thapar nor the ex–field director Fateh Singh Rathore could find them. Several tigers had also disappeared from Dudhwa.

In fact, the tigers were being poached but at first neither the authorities nor the international conservation community would believe it. In the spring of 1993 I started researching and writing a BBC film to be called simply *Tiger Crisis*. Both Claude Martin, Director General of WWF, and Arun Ghosh, Director of Project Tiger, were interviewed in the film and both doubted that tigers were in trouble. Tigers, after all, had been saved. But the film also featured the appalling horde of fresh tiger bones found in a store in the airless, oven–baked winding back streets of the walled town of Old Delhi by undercover agent Vivek Menon. He was working for Ashok Kumar and Traffic–India (ironically an off–shoot of WWF itself). The dark, dusty little warehouse crammed with skulls and skins was a shocking image. Menon had set up a sting, promising to purchase tiger parts from a Delhi–based Tibetan named Pema Thinley. At midnight on 30 August 1993 Menon went for his rendezvous, taking the police with him. They caught Thinley and a cohort called Yakob and with them they found 200 kg (440 lb) of tiger bones, some so fresh that the strands of meat were still attached.

It turned out that Tibetan refugees were smuggling the bones north into China. Traditional Chinese Medicine – practised all over the world, in London, New York and San Francisco as well as the back–streets of Shanghai – uses ground tiger bone as an analgesic. This is an ancient medical practice, indeed the anti–inflammatory effects of tiger bone have been tested and proven by Western scientific techniques, though other bones would probably have a similar mild usefulness. Meanwhile, Eastern beliefs ascribe all sorts of potency to the rest of the tiger's body parts. The fat is considered a cure for leprosy in

India, tiger claws are a sedative in Laos, the whiskers are used against toothache, the blood is taken as a tonic, the tail for skin diseases, the eyeballs for convulsions and cataracts. The end price for a tiger in 1993 was at least £4000 ($6000). It is nearer £10,000 ($15,000) now. But why the sudden climactic demand in the late 1980s and early 1990s? It's only a guess but the answer may well be that the stores of tiger parts derived from Mao's slaughter of 5000 or more tigers in the 1960s were exhausted and the market was looking further afield for supplies.

Whatever the case, Thinley and Yakob said all the bones had been collected since the previous monsoon and they could easily supply a further 1000 kg (2200 lb). A few days later, a raid on Delhi's Tibetan refugee camp produced another 87 kg (191 lb) and 200 kg (440 lb) were found nearby, along with the skins of six adult tigers, two cubs, 43 leopard skins, 128 otter skins and other assorted pelts. It all added up to a street value of £625,000 ($938,000). Since a single tiger yields between 10 and 16 kg (22–35 lb) of bone, the whole lot probably represented 30–40 tigers. It was by far the biggest haul of tiger bones ever seized and from the evidence gathered, Ashok Kumar concluded that at least 500 tigers had been poached in India in the previous three years. Menon, with his detailed undercover knowledge, believed the figure might be as high as 1000. Clearly, the world's tigers could not sustain such a level of persecution.

The mastermind, Yakob's relative Sansar Chand, escaped arrest at the time. His name was on the police blotters but no one seemed to know what he looked like, though he had initially been arrested for wildlife smuggling back in 1972 when the first animal protection laws came into force. His lawyers had managed to delay his case until 1982 when he had been given a jail sentence but released on bail. He was still out on bail in 1993! I followed his subsequent arrests, bails and dances in and out of India's courts through the pages of *BBC Wildlife Magazine* but at least his cover was blown.

The actual making of *Tiger Crisis* – badgering the authorities throughout 1993 – as much as its first screening in January 1994, probably marked a watershed in the world's perception of the poaching threat and the issue of Traditional Chinese Medicine. At the same time, on 1–3 September 1993, Delhi hosted the first ever meeting of the Global Tiger Forum, which most of Asia's tiger countries attended in order to co–ordinate research and stamp out poaching. WWF began to listen to the warnings emanating

Above: Tiger parts are common ingredients in Chinese medicine.
Opposite: Poached nilgai, Madhya Pradesh. Prey depletion is perhaps the most potent threat to tiger populations.

from their Traffic offices in the Far East and on 30 November it approved an emergency budget of £148,500 ($222,750) to update the information on the tiger bone trade in South Korea, China, Hong Kong, Yemen and Oman. Their researchers went on to produce some excellent reports, as did Mike Day and his Tiger Trust and the Environmental Investigation Agency (EIA).

Meanwhile, on 7 September 1993, US Secretary of the Interior Bruce Babbit threatened trade sanctions against China and Taiwan under the 'Pelly Amendment'. 'The United States cannot stand by,' said Babbit, 'while the world's remaining tigers and rhinos slip into extinction as a result of illegal commercial trade in the world marketplace. Our action today will send the message that unlawful trade in these rare species will not be tolerated.'

The sudden perception that there was a crisis also helped, by inviting donations and focusing public interest, to encourage the work of two outstanding small conservation organizations. Global Tiger Patrol has continued to channel funds to cost-effective initiatives, especially in and around India's National Parks. It has, for instance, helped to finance Raghu Chundawat's research in the dry forests of Panna in Madhya Pradesh and the water-harvesting projects spearheaded by Rajendra Singh in Rajasthan. Meanwhile, though Traffic-India eventually foundered, its undercover work was taken up by the Wildlife Protection Society of India and its director, Belinda Wright, who has supplied vital tip-offs to India's high–powered Central Bureau of Investigation (CBI), resulting in numerous recent busts.

One result of *Tiger Crisis* and pressure from its 'stars', Valmik Thapar, Ashok Kumar and Ullas Karanth, was that the Indian Government promised to set up an anti–poaching task force to combat poachers on the ground. This never happened. In April 2000, at the 11th meeting of CITES in Nairobi, India was singled out for particular and brutal criticism by the CITES Tiger Missions Technical Team.

It was therefore in answer to CITES and in some sort of fulfilment of the old promise that a new Tiger Enforcement Task Force, as part of an initiative to train officers from all 14 tiger nations, met in Delhi in April 2001, as was the granting four months earlier of special powers to the CBI to deal with animal–part smuggling.

Tiger Crisis highlighted the prediction that, were poaching to continue at the rate it was occurring in the early 1990s – one tiger per day – tigers might not make it into the twenty-first century. This was a sincere statement at the time and not a piece of sensationalism and, since poaching was subsequently reduced, we will never know what would have happened. Nevertheless, poaching has certainly not ceased – indeed at least 14 tigers were killed in India in the first 46 days of 2003 alone – yet numbers are relatively stable or anyway not in steep and irreversible decline. I now believe that, for several reasons, poaching of tigers, though very serious, is not the main threat to the species.

To some extent poaching imitates natural background mortality, resulting in more food and resources being available to the survivors. Furthermore, tigers are harder to find when they are persecuted. Consequently, the law of diminishing returns comes into play. The more tigers are poached, the fewer are left and the more difficult and expensive it becomes to pursue them. And provided protection measures remain in force, the poacher will face an escalating risk of being caught the longer he is forced to remain in the field searching for his quarry.

This is not to say that poaching doesn't matter. Chundawat has had three breeding radio–collared tigresses under observation in Panna for some years. The reserve is easily big enough to contain the home ranges of three females but they don't know that. Instead, they each have a small area of their range which extends beyond the protection of the park boundary where they are vulnerable. This was proved a few weeks before I visited Chundawat there to see his work in January 2003. His favourite female, who had rendered him so much fascinating data, was snared by villagers, leaving two nine–month old cubs who were most unlikely to survive. Chundawat was heartbroken. Six men were in custody, one of whom had been acquitted of tiger poaching just a month earlier.

Prey depletion: the real threat

Nevertheless, while poaching can cause serious haemorrhaging of the tiger population there is another even more insidious threat that really can wipe them out. A clue to what this is can be found in the fate of the three tiger populations that, within living memory, have become extinct. Until 1976 there were tigers in the Caspian region. According to V. G. Heptner and A. A. Sludskii, who examined the old records in detail, the last tigers in Kazakhstan did not live in jungles and they did not die out because the forests were destroyed. They inhabited reed beds in the river valleys east of the Aral Sea, using snaky threads of habitat, sometimes 1000 km (625 miles) long, where they rooted out wild boar. What finished them off was the poisoning of the boar population when the reed beds were converted to paddy fields. The same thing happened in Bali, where the last tiger disappeared less than 40 years after the subspecies was first described to

science by Schwarz in 1912. In Java the wild boars were poisoned to protect the newly established teak plantations. Tracks of three tigers were found there in the late 1970s and rumours of fresh scratches on trees persist but the last scats collected contained the remains of two mongooses, two porcupines, a bird and a palm civet – not a sustaining diet for a tiger. John Seidensticker wrote an elegiac article in *Tigers of the World* about the extinction of the tigers in Bali and Java entitled 'Bearing Witness'. He tracked those last stragglers on Java and concluded that the islands no longer had room for tigers but what his article actually tells us is that the tigers ran out of food.

In the spring of 1997 the Zoological Society of London hosted a symposium called 'Tigers 2000'. The papers, published as *Riding the Tiger,* included an elegant contribution by Dale Miquelle, Evgeny Smirnov and their colleagues from the Siberian Tiger Project. They examined the exact distribution of known tigers in the Primorski Krai region of the Russian Far East, comparing this with a wide range of variables, including several key habitat types. One variable fitted the tiger map like a glove – but with one finger missing. This was the distribution map for red deer. The missing 'finger' comprised a couple of small patches on the western fringe where there were tigers but few or no red deer. But when the map for wild boar was superimposed, lo and behold, the finger was filled. Tiger distribution did not precisely conform to any single preferred habitat but it followed very closely the distribution of main prey.

Two other excellent papers were delivered, one by Ullas Karanth and Bradley M. Stith entitled 'Prey depletion as a critical determinant of tiger population viability' and the other, 'Long-term monitoring of tigers: lessons from Nagarahole' by Ullas Karanth, Mel Sunquist and K. M. Chinnapa. Though they were based primarily on work from the opposite end of the tiger's geographical range they came to the same conclusions as the Russian study. The first paper used well-substantiated

mathematical models to show that a modest-sized tiger population could sustain low level poaching indefinitely since it meant there was more food left for the survivors. The depletion of prey, however, stressed the entire tiger community and had an immediate negative effect on females, depressing their carrying capacity, reducing cub survival and greatly increasing the risks of extinction.

The second Karanth paper was even more persuasive. It showed that specific conservation measures in Nagarahole had transformed tiger numbers since the 1970s. At that time the park had contained numerous villages and the deer and wild boar population was ravaged by poaching. They were shot and netted with dogs in the daytime and with lights at night. Wild boar in particular were snared or killed by baited explosives laid on forest trails, there was heavy loss to domestic dogs kept by the villagers in the park and there were even problems with people stealing predator kills. Between 1970 and 1990 many of these pressures were removed as people were resettled outside the park, disturbance was reduced, conflict over crop-raiding by ungulates diminished and poaching was actively discouraged. None of these measures was aimed directly at tiger conservation but the results were sensational. The numbers of breeding female tigers rose from 5 to 18, the densities of mature tigers increased from 2.3 to 8 per 100 sq km (38 square miles) and the overall population soared from 15 to 52.

Some older statistics are also relevant here. During George Schaller's 1964–5 study in Kanha he found that fewer than 25 per cent of the tigresses in his area were productive. When in 1979 H. S. Panwar published his own research from Kanha, as he found it in the late 1970s, he recorded a significant rise in productivity to 43 per cent. What had changed? Kanha had originally comprised a series of tiger-hunting blocks. When it was given reserve status in the 1950s it was primarily to protect, not tigers, but the endangered dryland subspecies of the barasingha, the beautiful 12-pointed swamp deer that had come close to extinction. But in the early 1970s Kanha became one of the first nine Project Tiger reserves and radical protection measures were enforced. These included the removal of 27 villages from within the park. The result: instant tiger productivity.

These observations tend towards an unfashionable conclusion. A recent dogma has grown up among international conservationists and has been incorporated into orthodoxy by the IUCN. It is called 'sustainable use'. The doctrine of sustainable use recognizes as legitimate the claims of indigenous people upon the economic resources of the forests, reserves or wildernesses in and around which they live. It appreciates, for instance, that the tribes of the Amazon rainforests or of Borneo have apparently lived for thousands of years in harmony with their environment, exploiting it in a sustainable way that does not reduce its overall productivity as a wild ecosystem. Building these interests into any long-term conservation strategy is a laudable political aim – both wise and just.

But while 'sustainable use' may be a sound principle, given the current state of tiger conservation, its application within our small tiger reserves would be plain daft. The idea of allowing people to troop back into the parks, cutting a bit of wood here, eating a deer there, grazing a few goats, is completely impractical. The resources to police it do not exist and the consequent degree of disturbance and destruction would be disastrous. For the moment the only way to protect tigers is to maintain (or if possible expand) the integrity of existing reserves while keeping all hunters, graziers, foragers and hewers of wood well outside the boundaries. The impressive increases in tiger productivity in Kanha and Nagarahole demonstrate the effectiveness of these old-fashioned policies.

It is clear then that the single most potent threat to tigers now is the loss of ungulates – the hoofed animals: deer, wild cattle, wild pigs, pachyderms (such as rhinos) – that comprise

their diet. In Thailand four out of six species of deer have disappeared. Cambodia has lost gaur, three species of wild cattle, elephants and the sambar. Even Chitwan, in Nepal, has seen its elephants, wild buffalo and barasingha depart in the last 50 years. This, rather than the direct persecution of tigers, is the unseen signature of destruction. In his provocative contribution to the film *Tiger Crisis* Karanth emphasized that tigers do not depend on woods and trees and that they cannot survive by eating grasshoppers. He has since coined the phrase 'love thy ungulate' to be a mantra for tiger conservationists.

Above: Part of a large haul of tiger skulls and bones found in Delhi in the early 1990s.

Conserving Tigers
Can We Save the Last 5000?

Palaeontologists tell us that the modern tiger appeared some two million years ago, probably somewhere in northern China or eastern Siberia. It was therefore a cold-climate animal with a heavy coat and the need to soak in water during the hot season in the tropical regions where it became most numerous. Indeed, as the species expanded its range, it had to adapt to a wide variety of landscapes and conditions, from the mountains and snow-line forests of the freezing north, down to the dense tropical forests of Malaysia and Indo-China, across the subtropical belt of riverine forests and grasslands in the foothills of the Himalayas until it reached those meandering reed beds near the Caspian.

Tigers also varied in appearance from region to region, the largest ones being most common in the Amur area of Siberia and the smallest and most densely striped on the islands of Sumatra, Bali and Java. Until 1997 these variations were deemed to represent eight distinct races or subspecies of tiger. These, from east to west, were thought to be the Amur tiger, the 'South China' tiger, the Balinese, Javan and Sumatran tigers, the Indo-Chinese tiger of Malaysia across to Thailand, the Bengal tiger of the Indian subcontinent and the Caspian tiger. In 1997, however, morphologist Andrew Kitchener looked at the evidence of size and colour differentiation between the 'subspecies' and showed that there was as much variation within them as there was between them and that while the biggest tigers were to be found in Russia and northern India, the size change was gradual and the result of standard climatic responses (larger size in colder climates) rather than geographical isolation. He concluded that there were probably only two races of tiger: the nominate (or typical) race and the Sunda Islands (Indonesian) tigers. These are generally smaller and have on average more than 26 stripes on the flank, whereas the nominate race averages 26 or fewer. But even within these separations he was talking averages, not invariables. More important, Joelle Wentzel and her colleagues at the US Laboratory of Genomic Diversity concluded in the same book *Riding the Tiger* that there was no persuasive DNA evidence for the existence of genetically separate subspecies of tigers. So for now it is accepted that a tiger is a tiger – or at most two tigers! This may seem like a purely academic argument but it does have important conservation implications.

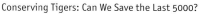

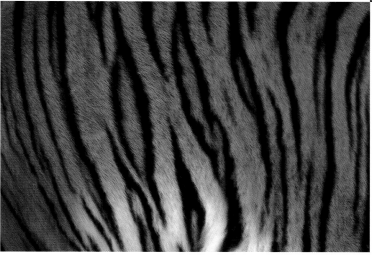

While the further loss of any population of tigers would be a tragedy, the possibility that there may be no distinct races means that all tiger populations are equal. Consequently, there is nothing irrevocable to be lost by concentrating scarce conservation resources on larger populations, which have the best chance of survival, rather than on the tiny ones that are most endangered. If, for example, the 'South China' tiger is a unique and irreplaceable subspecies, then one is inclined to throw large sums of money and effort into keeping it. If, on the other hand, it is just a scattering of 30 or so ordinary tigers (fewer than the population of a small Indian park like Panna), then it puts things into a different perspective.

This may be the place to mention the so-called 'white tiger'. White tigers too are not a discrete race. They are the result of a colour mutation that has occurred naturally but very infrequently in the wild in India. The colour is not generally advantageous and so, though in zoo specimens it is associated with large size, it has not established itself in nature. White tigers are not albinos. Albinos lack all pigment and have 'pink' eyes – pink because the lack of pigment in the retina makes the blood visible through the lining of the veins. White tigers have sooty stripes and pale blue eyes. These assets make them very attractive as zoo show-pieces and some of the most respected zoo curators, like Kailash Sankhala, have selectively bred them in captivity. For example, between 1970 and 1987 Cincinnati Zoo in Ohio, USA, bred 52 white tigers and this enthusiasm has generated some handy knowledge about the avoidance of excessive inbreeding. This could one day be useful in the sad event of tigers disappearing from the wild or needing serious reintroductory input from zoo

Opposite: Sumatran tigers are smaller and have more stripes than the main animal.
Above: The nominate race average 26 or fewer stripes; Indonesian tigers average more than 26 stripes.

sources. In the meantime, however, white tigers remain an interesting diversion rather than a conservation issue.

WWF biologist Eric Dinerstein has argued for an ecosystem approach to tiger conservation, dividing the tiger's range into discrete Tiger Conservation Units (TCUs). Every separate population of tigers that is effectively cut off from its neighbours is deemed to be a TCU. The small 350-sq-km (135-square-mile) parks of Sariska and Ranthambhore in Rajasthan comprise two TCUs, whereas the entire expanse of Russian Siberia – where in theory all the tigers can communicate with each other by passing through unbroken tiger terrain – amounts in effect to a single TCU. Obviously, some TCUs are more important than others. Dinerstein identifies roughly 160. Of these, 61 per cent are probably not viable; 86 per cent contain fewer than 25 breeding adults; and only a handful – perhaps six at most – are believed to contain the 50 or more breeding adults that biologists consider necessary to ensure a viable population in perpetuity. These are, probably: Siberia, the Sundarbans, the Kanha complex, the Corbett-Terai complex and its buffer zones and maybe the western forests in Thailand and perhaps Taman Negara in Malaysia.

This is why the question of whether there are 5000 or 7000 tigers left in the wild may not be the most important one. Perhaps the real issue is whether those mere half-dozen viable populations are sufficient, since they amount to just 1200 'safe' tigers. How can we best protect them and expand them and what chance do the tigers have in the smaller reserves and populations? Finally, what are the most valuable tools left in our tiger conservation kit and can tigers help themselves?

Let's take the last question first. Yes, tigers certainly can help themselves. The tiger is not a delicate species. It has shown itself adaptable to a wide range of habitats, so it is not vulnerable to the loss of some highly specialized biotope. It also has prodigious powers of recovery from persecution.

Survival in fragmented habitats?

The next question is whether tigers can really survive in all those small fragments of isolated habitat. Conservationists have traditionally worried about the impoverishment of the gene pool in small populations of rare animals. The biological mechanism for the distribution of fresh genes among tigers is the dispersal of the males. The further they can travel, the more likely they are to meet and mate with females that are unrelated to themselves and this ensures a healthy genetic turnover in the population as a whole. The problem now, of course, is that the males from these small tiger 'islands' are finding it harder and harder to disperse. Those that try have to cross open farmland and are likely to be poisoned or shot, or may even starve. This process selects in favour of the less adventurous males who stay at home and mate with mama or little sister.

In a human population this would cause a major crisis. Inbreeding is both a religious and biological taboo and our own justified fear of it has misinformed our understanding of animal genetics. Compared with most other animals, humans have a relatively high proportion of 'junk' genetic material, which emerges as deformity early on in a cycle of inbreeding. The Habsburg chin syndrome – by which the chins of the inbred

Habsburg royal family of the Austrian empire were reputed to have become so long that their owners couldn't eat properly – has always terrified conservationists. So far, however, chins among wild animals look pretty good because most animal species have very clean genetic profiles. Even where an isolated population is derived from a tiny number of individuals, genetic problems are usually absent. The Asiatic lions, for instance, were reduced to a tiny population at the end of the nineteenth century. Estimates varied from 70 to 12. Protection has helped them to recover to between 300 and 400, all living in and around the forest of Gir in Gujarat. This has involved an enormous amount of inbreeding yet the animals still appear to be clear of congenital disease or weakness. As a back-up conservation strategy, responsible zoos (like London Zoo) keep stud books to ensure as wide a distribution of Asiatic lion genes as possible – and some zoos do the same for tigers. But, again, though tigers are more prone to certain diseases in captivity than in the wild, the problem does not appear to be genetic so much as a product of captive conditions. Furthermore, in the United States alone, there are reckoned to be more tigers kept as pets than are left in the wild in Asia (a *Daily Telegraph* article in February 2002 estimated there were 15,000 privately owned tigers in the United States) yet no obvious gene problems seem to have emerged. Genetic degradation is probably not a short- or medium-term problem for wild tigers and we should therefore not be deterred from protecting even the smallest populations.

Another concern is that increasingly closely related tigers in isolated groups might gradually become less inclined to mate. We know that tigers can express preferences and that some like each other more than others. Researchers have also noted how the wolves of southern Sweden, all deriving from a single mating in 1983, were not keen to mate with siblings even from different litter years and that breeding there was only sporadic until a new male appeared from the north. Interestingly, wolves may have more of a

problem than tigers. Zoo wolves seem to be prone to occasional congenital blindness and we know that the selective breeding of dogs has led to enfeeblements such as hip displacement in German Shepherds. But tigers seem not to mind mating with their relatives. The more we know about individual tigers in these small reserves, the more interconnected they turn out to be. A tiger soap opera would be pretty strong stuff with incest between all family members forming the basis of most episodes.

Corridors of survival

Nevertheless, though small reserves are valuable and certainly better than nothing, there can be no doubt that large ones are better. So how can we help them to grow? One way is to join the reserves up. Half of India's tigers are said to live outside reserves

yet not much is known about them. There has been very little quality research into the way tigers use sub-optimal habitat. Dave Smith reported from Chitwan that tigers were unwilling to cross open cultivated land broader than a few kilometres, but this may have been a local phenomenon since alternative dispersal routes were probably available. V. G. Heptner and A. A. Sludskii noted that tigers had been recorded crossing the desert between northern Iran and the eastern Caspian shore and we know that tigers actually select sugar-cane fields round Dudhwa as birthing dens for their cubs. It may be that standing crops present no barrier to tigers on the move. The tigress that recently turned up at the famous bird reserve at Bharatpur in Rajasthan probably

Above: A tiger contemplates the degraded landscape outside Ranthambhore National Park in India.

Above: The tiger is considered to be sacred in India as
it is the steed of the Goddess Durga.

crossed miles of unsuitable terrain since the nearest main population is centred 200 km (125 miles) to the northwest in Sariska. Even more surprising, another stray tiger has now been found in the Sanjay Gandhi National Park on the very outskirts of Mumbai (Bombay). This is a subject that we need to know much more about because it could have a significant bearing on tiger conservation. If sub-optimal habitat is important to tigers, then we need to confirm this. We need to identify the areas most used, or most likely to be used, so that the information can persuade

politicians to offer tigers more protection. The obvious role of these habitats is as corridors between main centres of tiger population. Even if they do not hold enough prey to permit breeding, they could be very valuable as safe resorts for dispersing and transient animals. If young male tigers have somewhere to go, not only can they eventually invigorate distant groups of tigers, but by dispersing they reduce the feeding pressure on the home ranges of resident males. As we have seen, productivity in tiger society is greatly boosted by the presence of well-established resident males, which must have enough to eat without having to wander too far.

There is one place in the world where the infrastructure already exists for extending forest corridors to enlarge vastly the effectiveness of tiger reserves. This is Madhya Pradesh. It is still the most forested state in India. It is also one of the poorest, which means that economic development does not have to be reversed and in the future could be designed with tigers in mind. Land there is relatively cheap and if the local people in the more remote areas could see some economic advantage in encouraging tigers, they might accept the idea since more remunerative alternatives do not yet exist. The most important thing about Madhya Pradesh, however, is that it contains several of the best tiger reserves in the world. I have driven from Indravati Tiger Reserve in the east, across to Pench, up to Kanha and then on up through Bandhavgarh to Panna. Much of the route contains some form of degraded woodland that could be restored as corridors. These parks and their buffer zones already cover some 8000–10,000 sq km (3000–3860 square miles) of prime tiger habitat and tigers are breeding very successfully there. In January 2003 in Bandhavgarh there were three females with 10 cubs between them, all within a few kilometres of each other. In Kanha at the same time three tigresses and their cubs were using parts of the same meadow. Imagine what it would mean to join all these areas up more effectively. The tiger really would be saved for ever.

One policy would be for conservationists to buy strategically located corridor land. This is already being done in a very small way by people like Vini Singh near Panna. The only problem is that it may exclude local people from economic activity. If their land could be leased, however, they could become involved in tiger policing and would benefit directly from its success. Conservationists would pay the landowners and villagers a 'tiger rent'. This would be conditional on the corridor being maintained, the ungulates protected and the tigers allowed to use it without being persecuted. Under this sort of arrangement, anyone who poached or poisoned a tiger would come to be seen as a threat to the economic well-being of the whole community. If, on the other hand, the conservation body is the landowner – though this is the simplest solution – actions against the tiger are more likely to be regarded as a blow for democracy.

I believe that a concerted effort could achieve something like this in Madhya Pradesh. Frankly, conservation bodies all over the world have no trouble raising money to save tigers. When we made *Tiger Crisis* the charity cash tills were soon ringing. Tigers are the most charismatic and astonishing animals on earth. Every time a charity holds out one hand with a picture of a tiger in the other, people fill their fists with cash. Money itself is not the main problem. The problem is that most of the charities have no idea how to spend it honestly and effectively.

It is no accident that tigers have survived better in India than almost anywhere else. India is predominantly a Hindu country. Most Hindus are vegetarians – some 60 per cent of the population at least. This means that, unlike the charming people of Thailand, for example, they have not chomped their way through their entire deer population. The Judaeo-Christian tradition puts animals beneath the heel of humans. The Hindu religion has, at its heart, a true reverence for all forms of life and in India there persists a profound spirit of tolerance – even sometimes respect – for the god-force in nature. When I left

school in the 1970s there were supposed to be just over 400 million people in India; today we know there are over one billion. Yet in all its long history of civilization this teeming nation has retained almost its entire megafauna. While in Britain we are lucky to see anything bigger than a badger, India still has rhinoceroses – vigorously protected in Assam – elephants, tigers, lions, leopards, wolves and wild dogs, pythons and king cobras. The whole of Africa has just ten species of cat; India has 15. The only big animal it has lost in recent decades is the cheetah – an animal that is hard pressed throughout its range.

India is still the place where tigers will be saved. But action needs to be taken before the people's own deep ecological philosophy is eroded by their increasingly active participation in the global economy. The greatest obstacle is political. Unscrupulous politicians see the national parks as stacks and stacks of bank notes just waiting to be pocketed or dished out to buy votes. For the parks have sealed up valuable resources. They have gravel and minerals, even diamonds. They have land and trees and, most of all, water. To such people what value do tigers have in comparison? On 24 August 2002 the famous national park of Ranthambhore was overrun by local villagers armed with rocks and sticks, who poured into the park with their cattle – 10,000 head. Seventeen park rangers were injured, the water holes drunk dry and the tigers scattered; at least one female and her cubs were lost. This came at the end of a long drought when tempers were running high. But conservationists claim it was also deliberately engineered by two local members of parliament who wanted to get rid of the police chief and the park's director because these officials had opposed some of the politicians' more nefarious projects. Encouragingly, the crisis was peacefully resolved by the first intervention under a new central government initiative. On 9 May 2002 India's Supreme Court inaugurated a specialist body called the Central Empowered Committee to cut through red tape and deal directly with illegal encroachments on forest lands. This high-powered four-man team, chaired by P. V. Jayakrishnan, secretary to the Government of India, and including the respected conservationist Valmik Thapar, immediately pressurized the Rajasthan authorities to remove the trespassers. As soon as the politicians went against them, the villagers melted away.

The role of science and scientists

At the launch of Project Tiger in the 1970s there was a concentration of political will in India, from Indira Gandhi down, that was irresistible. At that time, most states as well as central government were of one mind and party (Congress I) so the Prime Minister's enthusiasm was infectious. This combination of political unity and energy is missing now. And there is another sort of grit in the mechanism. Tigers attract big egos, and big egos don't always work well together. It is utterly astonishing, for instance, that only two top-quality scientists are working on tigers in the whole of India. In Kanha, the best tiger reserve in the world, there is not a single piece of research being carried out – not even one on termites or flora. Nothing! This is a negation of the whole principle of Project Tiger, which was supposed to fund a scientific officer in every single Project Tiger reserve. One reason for this neglect appears to be that some people in authority are jealous of their own knowledge and believe that it cannot be bettered, so they block applications for scientific permits and funding. Every bureaucrat and desk-scientist who has spent a few days driving around the jungle sees himself (sometimes herself) as a tiger expert. When Raghu Chundawat was trying to initiate his now-influential research in Panna, he was told by a senior official that everything he would discover during years of research was already known and could be written down on a single sheet of A4 paper. In October 2001 I was honoured to give the seventh Kailash Sankhala Memorial Lecture in Delhi. I

mention this only because I took as my subject aspects of our ignorance of the natural world, the value of new science and the need for further research, especially on tigers. This was a disinterested plea since I was not asking for funds myself yet I encountered some ferocious criticism from people who thought they already knew everything worth knowing.

People have been laying down the law about tigers and what we know for more than 100 years. Yet in the course of writing this book I have come to appreciate the enormous contribution made by the most recent studies. This work, by Raghu Chundawat, Ullas Karanth and Dale Miquelle and the team in Siberia, has all been completed in the past decade. I have also come to realize that there is so much we do not know. For example, wouldn't it be interesting to do a DNA analysis of tiger scats found in those corridors and in the sub-optimal habitats between reserves? This would be an unobtrusive way of finding out which tigers were using them and where they had come from. It would then be useful to see whether any of the males are making it across to other parks away from their natal areas and managing to sire cubs. At the moment we assume we know which males father which cubs but it is pure guesswork. Scat analysis on lions in Botswana seemed to reveal a very different pattern of paternity from what the researchers had predicted. Perhaps we are getting it wrong in India, too. In the meantime, we still don't know whether or where successful dispersal is occurring, even though this has important implications for tiger conservation.

Active scientific field work is a vital conservation tool, even when it does not reveal any strikingly original information. The mere presence of an enthusiastic scientist in a reserve can be a tonic for the management. Ullas Karanth's long-term commitment to Nagarahole in Karnataka has been a support to a tough management team, led for many years by the outstanding park director K. M. Chinnappa. His research has given management the data they required to pursue vigorous anti-

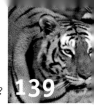

encroachment policies. It has also brought recognition and status to the forest staff and encouraged them to believe that their work has value. Finally, Karanth has involved local people, teaching them to count tigers and help with prey censuses, and this has led to a wider conservation education project. By establishing a network called 'Wildlife First' to co-opt local students and young people he was able to influence public opinion against poachers and wood smugglers, thus smoothing the way for more efficient enforcement of park regulations. And, as we have seen, tiger numbers in the park soared. Unfortunately, Nagarahole has experienced a bad spell recently, following Chinnappa's retirement. In 2002 a gang of tiger poachers was found operating deep inside the park, and in the last three years Wildlife First say that 77 elephants have been poached, 90 sq km (35 square miles) of the park burnt and nearly £1 million ($1.5 million) of timber smuggled out. One problem seems to be a vast loan from the World Bank's Global Environmental Facility, which has poured money into forest department hands for dubious rural development projects, thereby distracting them from their real tasks of policing the reserve. One hopes that Karanth's presence will eventually help to pull things back into shape.

A beneficial 'scientist' effect has certainly occurred at Panna in Madhya Pradesh. The involvement of Raghu Chundawat has already achieved surprising results in just eight years. His influence has helped the park managers to close down several mining works and illicit stone quarries, as well as providing them with a prey management plan. His vigilance in the field has been a deterrent to poachers, freeing forest staff for essential land-management work, and again tiger numbers have increased, from around seven to 32 today. Just one of his radio-collared tigresses has produced four litters of cubs and become the mother or grandmother of 26 new tigers. Every reserve can benefit from such a champion. Ranthambhore has had Valmik Thapar for 27 years; Chitwan has had Charles McDougal for more than 30; and

their influence and commitment have undoubtedly helped to keep the interests of those parks in the government eye.

Another essential bulwark of tiger conservation anywhere in the world is having the right forest officials in the most critical jobs. In India, park field directorships have sometimes been purely bureaucratic posts, even regarded by some ambitious appointees as a form of unwelcome exile away from the real and more lucrative heart of the Civil Service. This is a pity because they are vital roles and in the hands of people like Chinnappa in Nagarahole and Fateh Singh Rathore in Ranthambhore much can be achieved. Until Spring 2003, Ranthambhore had G. V. Reddy, reputed to be a man of real vision. He had recently pushed through gas connections to 9000 houses round the park, at a cost of £175,000 ($262,500). This may not look like a tiger issue but it is. Each connection may serve up to ten people; that means 90,000 people who will have less reason to enter the park and its buffer zones to cut fuel wood. Nagarahole, however, no longer has Chinnappa, and Reddy seems to have been forced out, too.

Valmik Thapar believes that the single most effective action that conservationists can take is to identify the best forest officers, support their promotion and defend them in their work. He argues that the Indian Forest Department already has everything in place to save the tiger if it wants to: it has the forests, it has the budget and it has the staff. If the right people are given command in the best reserves, and their management policies are not allowed to be undermined by politicians with alternative agendas, then India's tigers can hang on.

Thapar has been a major force in the Ranthambhore Foundation, set up by the far-sighted Peter Lawton, to tackle eco-development issues such as providing alternative fuels to villagers, improving their cooking equipment, introducing cattle with higher milk yields that can be stall-fed, and protecting their water supplies. Nevertheless, he feels that Non-Governmental Organizations (NGOs) have an indifferent record in India. This is perhaps a little harsh. American money – the Wildlife Conservation Society, supported by Exxon Corporation and the National Fish and Wildlife Foundation – has helped Karanth start his Karnataka Tiger Conservation Project in four top tiger habitats in the state, providing 20 patrol vehicles, three boats, wireless equipment, insurances and training for 1000 forest personnel. This is part of £1 million ($1.5 million) they have so far invested on tiger projects worldwide. Global Tiger Patrol has teamed up with London Zoo in at least seven tiger reserves in four states to finance insurance schemes for front-line anti-poaching staff, to supply vehicles and boats, to fund schools, hospitals and water projects for local communities and to help pay for Chundawat's research. Called 21st Century Tiger, this alliance has, since 1997, put £500,000 ($750,000) into field projects in Sumatra, Malaysia and Siberia, as well as India. Operation Amba, in Siberia, has seen some real success in co-ordinating anti-poaching activities there. Care for the Wild and the Environmental Investigation Agency have also made significant contributions, and in India there is a new blossoming of home-grown interest groups. Bittu Sahgal, the influential editor of *Sanctuary* magazine, has helped to start an educational movement called 'Kids for Tigers', which takes the message to schools all over the country. The Tiger Trust, founded in the name of Kailash Sankhala and associated with the tourist business, has finally started to fund the pursuit of tiger-poaching cases through the courts and there is encouraging evidence – even from the growth of the worldwide internet subscriber chatroom-site, nathistory-india@Princeton.EDU – that conservation issues are being taken seriously by more and more Indians. One small indication of burgeoning interest was a recent flamingo watch organized by the Bombay Natural History Society and the Bombay Port Trust. They invited interested parties to come and admire the 10,000 flamingos on the Sewree-Mathul Mudflats at 1500 hours on 17 May 2003. More than 1000 people turned up.

Ecotourism

It is true, however, that NGOs tend to embroider their successes when they are asking for funds and that the charity sector continues to be excessively fragmented and individualistic. The same applies broadly to the ecotourism industry, which has yet to deliver on its promises of significantly raising the standard of living for local people. Tourism does, however, contribute to tiger conservation in two important respects.

Firstly, the presence of tourists acts as a constraint on poachers. The fact that numerous vehicles are roaming over the national parks, containing people who are more or less committed to tigers continuing in the wild, amounts to a free patrolling service. Fear of what tourists may see or report also keeps forest managers up to the mark. If there are corrupt officers, willing to 'sell' illegal grazing and wood-gathering rights to villagers, or to involve themselves in more serious wood smuggling or even tiger poaching, then they are unlikely to pursue these activities under the noses of inquisitive visitors. This is not to say that forest services in any tiger country are institutionally corrupt. The Indian Forest Department has a proud record on the whole. But it is noticeable that in the areas of parks that are open to tourists the condition of the forest is often better than in the closed areas and the tigers thrive better. Some closed parts of Bandhavgarh – which is a well-managed park – are degraded in comparison with the Tala Range, the tourist area, and Tala has the highest density of tigers in the park. (The latest census found 64 tigers in the park's 448-sq-km (173-square-mile) core; 23 were in Tala, which covers just 96 sq km (37 square miles). I firmly believe that the tigers of both Kanha and Ranthambhore also gain safety from 'the tourist effect'.

The second benefit of tourism is that it brings status and recognition to a park and its staff. Kanha, for instance, even though it is eight hours' drive from Nagpur, the nearest large town, and lies in a remote part of a remote state, is not a

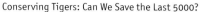

backwater. Its directors have traditionally moved on and up within the service. It is in fact essential that people see the parks, because they pay for them. In India, every vehicle crammed with people – even the noisy ones – spells hope for the tiger. I have met whole families in Kanha who have no special interest in wildlife but who have travelled all the way from Mumbai (Bombay) with small children just for the Diwali weekend. And they have seen a tiger and their lives have changed for ever. Because no one can see a wild tiger and not be changed – however slightly – by the experience. These people go home to the city where their friends have scoffed at their chances of spotting a tiger and they confound them. For Indians, seeing a tiger makes them proud of their parks and they and their circle will then be happier to spend their taxes on keeping them.

I admit that I used to find the presence of hundreds of other chatty people, zooming around Kanha when I wanted to watch tigers, thoroughly irritating, but an incident that occurred there a few years ago modified my opinion. It was mid-morning and we were trundling towards the headquarters in the park to check for news, when a jeep shot past in the opposite direction leaving the shout of 'leopard' in its dust. We turned and followed it, rounded a corner and hit a traffic jam. There must have been 50 vehicles there. I'd had no idea there were that number in the entire park. They were squeezed together at every angle like crazy-paving and everyone was gesticulating towards a patch of trees on a knoll to the right. At first I was horrified but after a quarter of an hour it dawned upon me that no one was shouting or quarrelling or pushing for a closer view. Instead, they were quietly trying to make room for everyone and show each other the leopard. She was very difficult to see and, though they all waited patiently, many of them could not spot her. Eventually everyone drifted away and after ten more minutes, when ours was the only jeep left, the leopard rose, stretched and wandered off into deeper cover. A lot of people had had an exciting morning, with no real harm done.

Above: The pressing need for fuel wood is a major factor in deforestation in India.

There is a movement among India's conservationist elite further to restrict what visitors are allowed to see and where they can go, on the grounds that they disturb the tigers. In particular they criticize the use of elephants to shuttle dozens of people in to photograph a tired tiger that may have been tracked for some hours. But this is a short-sighted attitude. You don't convert people by banning them. It would be better instead to try to ensure that every visitor gets the best possible experience. Ask them to be quiet and respectful and enforce a more rigorous set of rules with the elephants. For most people an elephant ride represents by far the best chance of seeing a tiger, so don't deny them. Just ensure that the elephants don't push too close. A tiger that is nervous and uncomfortable with an elephant-load of tourists 4 m (13 feet) away will relax when that distance is doubled.

There are 'deeper' environmental objections to tourism: for example, that unnecessary aeroplane journeys are hideously polluting the upper atmosphere and that tourists strain the infrastructures of the places they visit, using up the ground water and leaving piles of non-biodegradable rubbish. To some extent these problems are inevitable. Even so, the benefits of tourism

outweigh the disadvantages – provided that the businessmen who rake in the cash are kept on their eco-toes and that development is minimized. It would be hard to defend the sort of mass tourism that has gobbled up the Mediterranean coast of Spain and turned much of Hawaii into a rich person's holiday camp.

So far, tiger tourism has not done much for local economies. It has provided a few low-level jobs, and some more conscience-stricken operators have tinkered with aid schemes, but in most tiger countries it does not yet make much of a contribution to the real costs of conservation, other than in the valid but indirect ways I have outlined above. A study by Marnie Bookbinder and others in the late 1990s found that very little of the £2.6–3.3 million ($4–5 million) earned each year by hotels in and around Chitwan in Nepal, for instance, found its way into the pockets of local families. Out of 87,000 workers there, only 1100 were employed in any way in ecotourism. Chitwan does, however, provide at least one model for a local self-help scheme that is worth exploring. In 1989 a modest USAID grant of £6650 ($10,000) led to the fencing of a 32-ha (79-acre) plot of government land at Bagmara, in the Chitwan buffer zone northwest of the village of Sauraha. It was planted with native rosewood, khair and other trees to provide timber and fuel wood and a wildlife habitat. In 1993 legislation in Nepal allowed the setting up of locally elected User Group Committees (UGCs) to manage such buffer-zone forests and share the benefits throughout the local community. Between 1994 and 1996 the Bagmara Community Forest expanded to cover 450 ha (1111 acres) and the UGC, elected by 584 households, worked with WWF to establish nature trails, build hides, excavate water holes and employ villagers as anti-poaching guards. Bagmara is important because, if it is successfully protected, it provides a link between the main park and the woodlands of Tikoli to the north, which are believed to be a potential corridor for tigers heading for the foothills of the Himalayas. According to Eric Dinerstein, who has

been a key figure in this project, by November 1995 Bagmara was ready to welcome tourists and during its first year of operation, up to October 1996, hosted 10,632 visitors who paid a whopping £192,000 ($276,432). In return they enjoyed well-organized elephant rides along carefully planned routes where they could see rhinos, crocodiles and even tigers. By July 1997, with the addition of another community forest at Kumrose, east of Sauraha, an area of 16.5 sq km (6⅓ square miles) had been fenced for regeneration. Not a single dead tree was taken during 1998 and illegal firewood collection has stopped completely. Grassland was fenced to exclude cattle and use of the area by tigers increased from zero to five tigers, including a female with cubs. At the same time 11 rhino calves were born there.

Bagmara and Kumrose have to share their revenues with Chitwan National Park but under the 1993 legislation this is reciprocated. Half of all park entry fees and hotel concession fees go direct to the park and these are then split 50:50 with the local community. In 1995–6 the park's share before this division apparently totalled £568,222 ($852,333). In a region where the average family's income is under £100 ($150) this is a considerable sum.

Dinerstein emphasizes that this is not a model for conservation within parks. There he agrees that strict protection policies and the exclusion of all unrelated economic activity are essential. But if wider landscapes are to be preserved to enable tigers to disperse or traverse them then some sort of economic benefit must accrue to local people to offset the short-term advantages they would have enjoyed through grazing, wood gathering and poaching. He concludes: 'Nothing short of major revenue-sharing schemes between parks and communities will guarantee the persistence of tigers occupying the larger landscapes or using dispersal corridors between core areas.' Chitwan has suffered reversals recently. The rise of Maoist rebels has distracted the army, which had hitherto been an effective

police force in the park, and some 31 rhinos were reported poached in 2001–2. Tigers may also have suffered, though statistics on them are harder to come by. But this is an extraordinary political setback that in no way negates the value of the Bagmara/Kumrose experiment. If eco-development is guided by honest brokers into the hands of local communities, it can provide a blueprint for the expansion of reserves outside their core protection areas, for the development of buffer zones and for the provision of corridors anywhere in the world.

Below: Elephant grass burning in Kaziranga National Park. Such management is supposed to encourage new shoots and better grazing for ungulates.

Managing national parks

Raghu Chundawat's research shows that it is not enough to protect core areas of parks. It is also important to discourage poaching and snaring outside – where other controls have to be relaxed – because even tigresses with cubs don't stick to park boundaries. Panna, where he is working, is a small park, but the principle applies even in very large parks. The Serengeti's 14,500 sq km (5600 square miles) proved too small to save the wild dog from the ravages of distemper and rabies picked up from village dogs on the western border. Even more relevant to tigers is Andy Loveridge's work on lions in Hwange National Park in Zimbabwe. There, male lions are shot as trophies by licensed recreational hunters who operate all round the park edge. The male

population has been decimated over the past ten years. Whereas previously a male coalition of two or three individuals would consort with a single female pride, now each coalition must divide its attentions between six prides. This means that the males travel all the time, visiting their females. There are fewer and fewer males to act as stops, so their journeys take them from the heart of the park to the boundaries in a radius of 80 km (50 miles), with the result that none of them is safe. Consequently, a vast park covering 15,000 sq km (5790 square miles) is no longer an effective refuge for lions at all. Boundaries without friends on the outside are no good in the long term.

Just as a large reserve does not guarantee security unless it is effectively policed inside and out, so a large tiger population is

not, in itself, a guarantee of long-term viability. What is most important in a tiger reserve is not the total number of individual tigers wandering within its perimeters but the number that are actually breeding. The key role for tiger reserves today must be to provide optimum conditions in which tigers can meet, mate and rear their cubs. The dispersal of the surplus beyond the boundaries is the next priority but it is not the first. Tigers breed freely when four conditions are met. First, there must obviously be the required number of eligible adults of both sexes within meeting distance of each other. Second, they should be as little disturbed as possible. Third, there should be stable male residents and as little conflict as possible between them. Finally, there must be a constant supply of suitable food, water and shade and it must be easily accessible from the safest denning areas.

The first three conditions can largely be met by traditional protection methods. In Panna, for instance, improved policing during the 1990s saw a marked reduction in disturbance, a rise in the number of eligible adults and the establishment of three resident males. Because these males were not poached or harassed, they maintained stable ranges and protected their own offspring. Consequently, tiger numbers increased from seven to 32 within eight years. The one area where new management ideas might be most helpful is in maximizing prey populations. As we know, a tigress rearing small cubs does not want to travel far to find something for them to eat, so any way in which park managers can encourage ungulates to concentrate in the safest core areas of their parks could be valuable. The basic tool is habitat management. If you want sambar, you encourage the growth of understorey for browsing. If you want chital, you create small glades and clearings, burning the cover to bring on new grass growth. If you want nilgai, you create larger open areas. Making the right choice is crucial, for a mistake could be disastrous.

This is a subject that Raghu Chundawat has been studying in Panna. Over the next few years, as his work progresses, it will

prove extremely influential, but already he points to certain broad conclusions. Panna is a dry tropical forest with a mixture of closed browsing, woodland glades and more open scrubland and these habitats support healthy populations of sambar, chital and antelopes, including nilgai. Chundawat has noticed, however, that although nilgai are nearly as large as sambar and should be ideal tiger food, they do not feature proportionately on the tiger's menu. This is because, like the other antelopes found in the park – chinkara for instance – they have evolved as open-ground animals. They feed away from good stalking cover, relying on sharp sight and a fast turn of speed to protect them from tigers. Their metabolism also helps them cope with the lack of shade in the hot summers. This the tiger cannot adapt to. Tigers, as we know, thrive in temperatures that vary from -38°C (-36°F) to 48°C (118°F). But they must have shade. In a place like Panna they simply don't use the open scrub during the summer, so however many nilgai there are, they are of little use to the tigers at that season. This, incidentally, gives us a clue to the geographical separation of lions from tigers. The lions of Gir in Gujarat eat a lot of nilgai because they are rather better adapted to open scrub forest: they have thinner, paler coats and they evolved largely as a savannah, rather than a deep-forest, hunter. Clearly, then, managing a tiger reserve for nilgai in the belief that you would be maximizing meat on the hoof would be a mistake. Chundawat believes that the best prey species to encourage may be chital. Sambar are the tiger's preferred meal but they apparently reach saturation point in Panna at six individuals per sq km (⅓ square mile). Chital can reach 13 per sq km (⅓ square mile) and, at current stocking levels, Chundawat believes there is the potential to quadruple their numbers in the park. Managing the reserve for chital could make a substantial difference to the

tigers of Panna, both in the number that breed and in their ability to raise the subsequent cubs.

This research reminds us how important it is to study tigers in every major location, how prescient it was for the founders of Project Tiger to prescribe a scientific officer in every reserve, and how sad it is that not a single park has one. Maximizing prey, however, is not necessarily a panacea for all the tiger's problems. Chundawat has shown that males and females have a different feeding agenda. He followed a tigress for six months and found that 80 per cent of her kills were wild prey, whereas a male during the same period killed 84 per cent cattle. His home range at the time was enormous – at 243 sq km (94 square miles), some ten times as large as hers. Consequently, he was too busy searching the terrain for other females to bother about where he picked up his dinners, whereas she had selected a smaller area, rich in undisturbed prey, where she could rear her cubs.

Although good management in the future will be able to increase the amount of natural prey in the parks, tigers will probably always take livestock and the goodwill and co-operation of local people will remain an essential ingredient in any tiger recovery plan.

Opposite: Dancer in costume at tiger festival, Udipi, India.
Above: Wall painting of tiger at Diwali festival, Mahu, India.

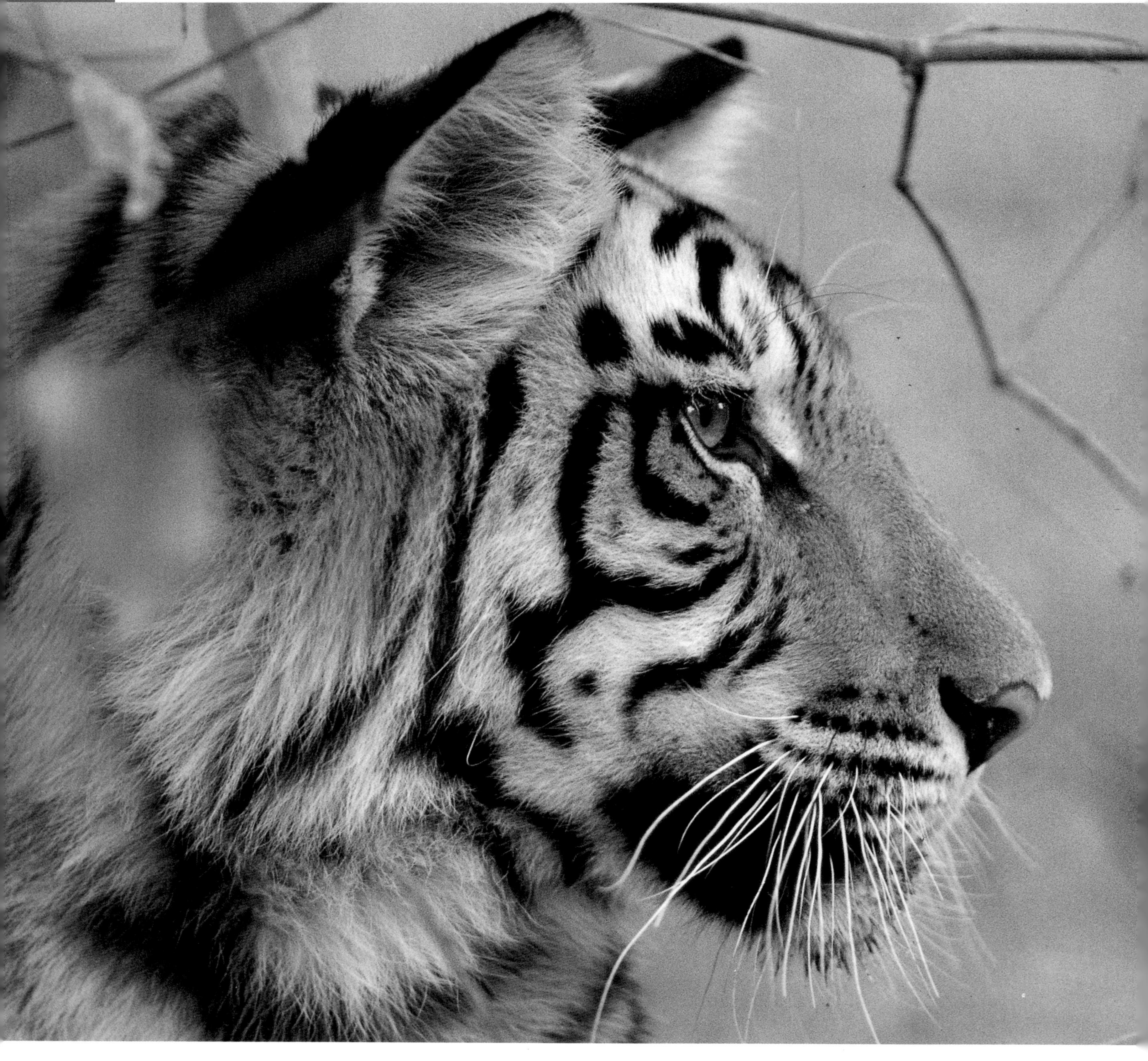

Where are tigers still to be found?
Which locations offer visitors the best chance of
actually seeing them?
Which are the best parks and reserves to visit?
Where are the best places to stay?
Advice on tracking and watching tigers.

Tiger Watching
How and Where to Find Tigers

There are only two countries in the world where you can seriously expect to see a tiger. These are
India and, to a lesser extent, Nepal. Other areas, like the Russian Far East and Sumatra, still have
substantial tiger populations but these are difficult to see. In the remaining nine tiger-range
states even researchers rarely spot one. Nevertheless, people are now eager to stray off the beaten
track; countries like Cambodia, Vietnam and Laos are beginning to open up for tourism and those
of you who are interested in tigers should go and look for them.

In many of these nations, tiger studies are in their infancy and I believe there is still a role for the serious amateur naturalist armed with binoculars and a notebook. If nothing else, the arrival of interested foreigners may help to put a tiger site on the map. When local people meet a visitor who has travelled halfway round the world to admire their forests and their wildlife, they are likely to reassess the value of those assets. At the same time the forest staff and volunteers who work in remote areas are often isolated. The arrival of enthusiasts from abroad can be a huge encouragement, conveying status on their work and helping to attract attention and funds to what they do. It may also open lines of communication and friendship that can be supportive.

The purpose of this final chapter, then, is to encourage you to look for your own tigers. Some scientists may be dismissive of the contribution that amateurs can make but until we know exactly how many tigers there are in the world and exactly where

they are, this attitude is ignorant. If you really can learn to distinguish between the footprints of tigers, leopards and leopard cats and you are prepared to photograph and record your evidence accurately, then there are organizations that may welcome your observations. A leader in this field is the Wildlife Conservation Society (WCS) but the World Wide Fund for Nature (WWF) and the Environmental Investigation Agency (EIA) also have a keen interest in tigers.

In the directory that follows I have tried to give some guidelines as to how and where to find tigers, describing at least one location where tigers are found in every range country. This is not a tour guide, so the suggestions for visiting are merely supposed to get you started. Some journeys founder because people simply don't know where to begin. Similarly, I have provided at least one potential first point of contact in each country. These are all people with whom I have been in touch and whom I have found to be helpful or informative. I am not, however, endorsing them or suggesting that they are the best contacts available. Furthermore, some are field workers who may be too busy to answer casual queries. There are also, for instance, dozens of

excellent tour providers specializing in India and I mention only a few because I know them personally. Finally, remember that the political situation in some of these countries is not stable. Travellers should get advice from their own governments before visiting these. At the time of writing, Sumatra contains trouble spots and many people might disapprove of visiting Myanmar.

Nevertheless, a glimpse of a tiger, say in Vietnam, might be a valuable record and it would be exciting if travellers took time out of normal tourism to lend support to tiger conservation in remoter countries. But if all you want to do is see one good tiger before you die - and everyone should - then start in India. Nowhere else looks after its tigers so well and nowhere else offers such a rich promise of success.

FIRST CONTACTS:

Useful introductory websites include: www.5tigers.org and the WCS at www.wcs.org

21st Century Tiger is currently updating a database listing all known tiger conservation projects. It is being co-ordinated by Sarah Christie at London Zoo and is expected to be up and running by the middle of 2004. Information will be available then from the Cats Specialist Group of the IUCN.

Left: A tigress with four grown cubs showing off in Ranthambhore National Park.

Finding your own tiger

Tigers are extremely difficult to see in almost all the places where they are still found. It is no disgrace to spend weeks looking for one and to fail. I spent eight months in the field during a two-year period in Kaziranga National Park, and though it has one of the highest densities of tigers anywhere in the world, I only saw a tiger once for approximately one millisecond.

I was making a film about rhinos at the time, so I could not follow up on tiger clues. You, however, can improve your own chances by exercising some basic skills. Tigers have soft sensitive pads to their feet, so they regularly use forest paths and sandy stream beds where they can travel quickly and

Below: Fresh tiger prints or pugmarks lie on top of previous tyre treads.

painlessly. In soft soils they leave tracks or 'pugmarks'. These are huge, consisting of a roughly triangular palm print (or pad) topped by four spread toes. A male's print is bigger than a man's hand and nearly as broad as it is long. A female's print is noticeably narrower and the toes are often closer together and more forward-pointing. Size is important. Any pad solitary and smaller than 6.5 cm (2½ inches) across is most likely a leopard, since a tiger cub would probably not be alone.

The age of the print is also a helpful clue. A print on top of a wheel track is obviously more recent than the passage of the car that left the track. A dry print after rain is more recent than the rain. Wet tracks on a dry road indicate that the tiger has just emerged from wet grass. Fresh tracks are always worth following. I was recently alerted to a tiger hiding in nearby bushes by a print with a single drop of dew in it. The dew was dripping from the leaves above and, even after a few minutes, the print would have been quite wet.

Prints are the most obvious indication that tigers are present but on hard ground they are not always visible, in which case it is worth looking for other signs. Tiger droppings, or scats, are large – 3–4 cm (1–1½ inches) broad and up to 20 cm (8 inches) long. They are often coiled and placed in a conspicuous place, like the grassy median of a track or on rocks. When fresh they are usually dark and smelly. They contain a lot of hair and this is more obvious

Above: Crossing the Rapti River in Chitwan, Nepal.

as they dry out in the heat. An old scat turns hard, desiccated and grey. In the monsoon scats are washed away within days, even hours, but in the dry season they can last for months. When urinating, tigers sometimes scrape parallel marks with their hind feet in the ground. These can remain after the urine has dried. They also leave deep scratch marks on the trunks of trees. They prefer trees with soft barks like the mahua (*Madhuca indica*), which bears a delicious little yellow fruit in April, much beloved of sloth bears, and has a brown trunk; or the pale-trunked arjuna (*Arjuna terminalia*). The marks are deep parallel furrows, usually showing three or four claws, and can be 1.8–2.4 m (6–8 feet) up. Sloth bears also make marks but usually not so high and closer together. Another animal that removes bark is the porcupine, not that its depredations could be confused with a tiger's. It gnaws a neat ring 6–8 cm (2¼–3 inches) broad and almost all the way round, starting just a few centimetres off the ground.

Another more arresting indication that tigers are around is the roar. Since lions and tigers no longer overlap, the only animal that can easily be confused with a tiger is probably an elephant. The elephant's roar is huge, with a screamy feel to it, and lacks the guttural edge of a tiger's roar. Leopards, on the other hand, make a rhythmical, raspy sound like a saw cutting through wood. The tiger's other calls – none of them very frequent, I'm afraid – are mostly recognizable as those of a big cat: mewing and moaning sounds. The one misleading call is the hollow 'pook' sound, which I have occasionally heard a tigress make to her cubs.

The most important sounds to listen for when searching for tigers, however, are the alarm calls they provoke from other forest animals. The progress of a tiger on the move will often – though not always – be signalled by a relay of alarms as it passes through one part of the jungle to another. Peacocks make a short trumpet sound, jungle fowls have a double cluck, langurs cough and muntjaks give a loud roaring bark. None of these is an assured indication of a tiger. The birds will react to a large bird

of prey, and monkeys are particularly frightened of leopards because, unlike tigers, they climb trees terrifyingly fast. The clue is that monkeys usually go on coughing for as long as they can see a leopard, whereas they generally stop when a tiger sits down. More reliable is the call of the chital, a short, pretty, high-pitched whistling bark, like someone calling 'whoo'. Sometimes, however, chital can react to you and so, if you can see them, check where they are looking. In April 2003 the Scandinavian film-maker Arne Naevra and I were puzzled one morning when one of Kanha's best trackers came out into the forest wearing a striped T-shirt. When he got out of the jeep to check the ground, the chital thought he was a vertical tiger and continued to alarm at us for 20 minutes. Barasingha have a desperate-sounding alarm somewhere between a bark and a gasp

but the most reliable witness of all is the sambar. It makes a short, loud, echoey trumpet call, not quite a cough or a bark.

The calls may tell you a tiger is there and in which direction it is travelling. If the calls continue, then it is probably still moving and if you know which stream bed or trail it is likely to be using, you can try second-guessing it. Using other roads to position yourself properly, you can have the tiger walk right out on top of you. For the layman, however, such techniques are only likely to work in a handful of reserves where there are plenty of paths and the tigers are not disturbed by the noisy mistakes you make. In most other places you will have to apply your skills with great delicacy.

Below: Male tiger in Kanha, Mukki region.

Country-by-country guide to watching tigers

India

Visiting Indian tiger reserves

Indian reserves offer by far the best chance of seeing tigers but they function very differently from, for instance, African reserves and this can come as a shock. Most do not open their gates until after sunrise and close before sunset. This means that, unless you have special privileges, you will lose some of the most precious time at dawn and dusk. At Kaziranga in Assam, tourists in vehicles would not be allowed in until after 7.30 a.m. The rhinos people had travelled there to see would mostly have disappeared into the long grass by then, leaving only a few stragglers for the visitors to watch. On one occasion I counted no fewer than 82 rhinos feeding in short-grass meadows at 7.00 a.m. By 7.30 a.m. only three were left. This is a frustration you just have to put up with.

Outside the gates of the most popular parks a pre-dawn queue of revving vehicles forms and this can be depressing for the solitary naturalist inclined to peace and quiet. But India has one billion people and many of them like to visit their own parks. In some ways the more that visit, the better, so please adapt.

Once inside, some people tear around looking for other people who might have seen something. Sometimes they bump into each other. My jeep was once nearly knocked into a pond in Bandhavgarh when the car behind us used us as a brake. But you don't

have to behave like this. With a little patience you can find reasonable solitude. In April 2003 Arne Naevra and I spent many hours over several days waiting quietly at a water hole in Kanha. An occasional jeep passed us but they saw nothing to stop for and left us alone. We were rewarded by two wonderful sights of a mother sloth bear and her cub and a beautiful tigress.

India is special. In India people like to talk. All the time. Because they sometimes see tigers while they are chatting – in fact I was once so busy talking myself that I didn't see a tiger until it had almost walked into the back of my jeep – people assume that talking doesn't matter. It does. You never know what you are missing until you shut up. Last April Arne and I were waiting in Chakradhara meadow in Bandhavgarh. The tourist vehicles were full of chatterers but because we were filming we had a half-hour extension in the park. As dusk fell the last jeep drove off and just two minutes later a tigress with four cubs walked right out in front of us to be filmed.

Very few Indian reserves permit you to sleep in the park. Instead, most have a variety of lodges near the perimeter. The famous parks are serviced by a sufficient range to suit all pockets. Backpackers with plenty of time at their disposal can make their own way to the park, find a modest village house to stay in and wait around to buy a spare place in a vehicle. The better-off can stay in the fairly decent state-run guest houses or there are usually some up-market

lodgings where your entire visit will be arranged for you. These generally have to be booked in advance, either through a tour operator or through offices in Delhi, Mumbai (Bombay) or Madras. With rare exceptions – for instance, lodges run by the Taj group – these do not offer the luxury of African safari camps but they have their own curious charms. In one decaying maharaja's palace, for example, I witnessed an unofficial court as the villagers squatted in a quiet line in the corridor waiting for their disputes to be resolved by the family that had once ruled them.

1	Kanha	10	Kaziranga
2	Bandhavgarh	11	Sundarbans
3	Panna	12	Royal Chitwan
4	Ranthambhore	13	Royal Bardia
5	Nagarahole	14	Sukla Phanta
6	Bandipur	15	Jigme Dorji
7	Mudumalai	16	Jigme Singye
8	Corbett	17	Manas
9	Dudhwa	18	Thrumshingla

FIRST CONTACTS:

Manoj Sharma, Tiger Resorts Pvt. Ltd
(Dynamic Tours Indian Nature Expeditions),
206 Rakesh Deep, 11 Commercial Complex,
Gulmohar Enclave, New Delhi 110049

    Tel. 91 11 26853760; 26516770,
26858656; Fax 91 11 26865212;
Email pradeep@tigersindia.com or
dynamictours@yahoo.com

Toby Sinclair and Suhail Gupta, Wild India –
Media Support and Travel, S-36 Panchsheel
Apts., A-1 Panchsheel Enclave,
New Delhi 110017

    Tel. 91 11 2649 7249; Fax 91 11 2649
7260; Email toby_sinclair@vsnl.com or
suhailgupta@vsnl.net

Vishal Singh, Royal Expeditions Pvt. Ltd,
R 184 Greater Kailash Part-1,
New Delhi 110048

    Tel. 91 11 26238545; Fax 91 11 26475954;
Email vishal@royalexpeditions.com or
royalexp@vsnl.com

UK:

Liz Drake, Spencer Scott Travel Services Ltd,
3 Cromwell Place, London SW7 3JE

    Tel. 44 207 225 2988; Fax 44 207 581
9109; Email info@spencerscott.com

Julian Mathews, Discovery Initiatives Ltd,
The Travel House, 51 Castle St,
Cirencester, GL7 1QD

    Tel. 44 1285 643333;
Email julian@discoveryinitiatives.com

Madhya Pradesh

Madhya Pradesh is the capital of the tiger's world. Until its recent subdivision it was the largest state in India, lying at the remote heart of the subcontinent and containing more than one-third of the nation's forest cover. The official 2001–2 tiger census recorded 710 tigers here, nearly twice as many as in any other state. The region has nine national parks. One of these, Sanjay, covers 1935 sq km (747 square miles) and is the biggest park in India. Five others – Kanha, Bandhavgarh, Indravati, Panna and Pench – are especially noted for their tigers and, while all are worth visiting, Kanha and Bandhavgarh are probably the best places to see tigers anywhere on Earth.

Below: Bandhavgarh Plateau, Bandhavgarh National Park, Madhya Pradesh, India.

KANHA NATIONAL PARK

Project Tiger Reserve 940 sq km
(363 square miles)

Kanha is reckoned to be one of only five places in the world where the tiger population exceeds 50 breeding adults, the figure required to ensure future viability. Tall sal forest in the northwest, watered by streams and swamps, gives way to open meadows in the south and this varied topography supports other rare animals like wild dog, wolf, gaur and a subspecies of barasingha that was saved from extinction by the founding of the park in 1955.

    In the area open to tourists some tigers are tracked by elephant and shown to visitors in the mornings. An orderly queuing system operates, which jeep drivers will understand. For some visitors, expecting a wilderness experience, this can feel a bit

like a trip to the zoo. You are allocated a number, told to wait in a car park and then given the signal to find the elephants and take your ride. But the tigers don't see it that way. They are wild. My friend Tarun Bhati had the bottom of his shoe torn by a tiger that leapt up at his elephant. So if you are lucky enough to see a tiger, don't take it for granted. It's always a privilege. The park is also criss-crossed with forest tracks and if your driver explores these carefully you have an excellent chance of finding your own tiger.

Visiting: best reached by internal flights to Nagpur (then seven hours by road) or by plane or train to Jabalpur (then six hours by road). Booked lodges can arrange road transfers.

Kanha has two main gates, Kisili in the centre west and Mukki in the south. Both have numerous tourist lodges and vehicles for hire nearby. There is a state rest house (Baghera Log Cabins) at Kisili. The more up-market lodges, like Kipling Camp and Wild Chalet Lodge at Kisili, and Kanha Jungle Lodge and Royal Tiger Resort at Mukki, and their vehicles need to be booked in advance.

BANDHAVGARH NATIONAL PARK
Project Tiger Reserve 448 sq km
(173 square miles)

Bandhavgarh has only half the number of tigers that Kanha has but they may be easier to see. Once the hunting preserve of the Maharaja of Rewa, this is an extremely pretty reserve, with 22 hills, a 2000-year-old fort, mixed forests with stands of bamboo, small meadows and reedbeds and a plentiful supply of ground water. The park entrance is at the village of Tala, and though it can seem crowded at holiday times, the tigers mostly ignore the vehicles and you would be unlucky not to see a tiger during a three-day visit. Patience and a good guide or driver can make a big difference here because the tigers are sometimes quite predictable. With my friend Vivek Sharma I recently trailed an invisible tiger for 6 km (3¾ miles) while we worked out what we thought he was doing. We then waited for an hour on the track ahead and he eventually emerged from the forest within 15 m (50 feet) of where we thought he would come. Tigers are also tracked for morning viewings by elephant, as in Kanha, and elephants can be hired for random walks in the afternoons. These are not often successful but to find your own tiger by elephant is very exciting and always worth a go. Bandhavgarh was made famous by the presence of one male, Charger, that held a home range there until he was 17 years old and, so honoured did he become, that he has his own burial place at 'Charger point'. He was named for his habit of charging at vehicles and, though his three grandsons now control his area, it was one of his daughters who inherited the inclination to intimidate jeeps. Sadly, this seems to have cost her her life. She was believed to have been hit by a car on the main road in March 2003 and, after making a desperate and inept attack on a tourist vehicle, she was never seen again.

Visiting: overnight train from Delhi to Katni (two to three hours by road) or Umaria (45 minutes by road). Alternatively, fly to Khajuraho (famous for its wonderful erotic statues) and then six hours by road. Seven hours by road from Kanha.

Reliable lodges include the state-run White Tiger Lodge, Churat Kothi (formerly Bandhavgarh Jungle Camp) and Bandhavgarh Jungle Lodge. The last two are more expensive but very pleasant.

PANNA NATIONAL PARK
Project Tiger Reserve 543 sq km
(210 square miles)

Panna is less well known but is very interesting for several reasons. Firstly, it has been the location for Raghu Chundawat's tiger ecology studies, during which tiger numbers have risen from single figures to more than 30. It is also a dryland tropical forest, which means that it supports a different array of ungulates from the more famous, moister parks. It has good populations of antelope – blue bull (nilgai), four-horned antelope (chowsingha) and Indian gazelles (chinkara) – as well as plenty of sambar and chital. Finally, it is very close to Khajuraho, so offers the chance to mix culture and tigers with relative ease. If you manage to make contact with any of the researchers your chances of seeing tigers

Above: Padam Talao, the 'first lake', with Ranthambhore fort in the background, Ranthambhore National Park, Rajasthan, India.

may be enhanced. In any case, a visit lasting several days offers reasonable odds.

Visiting: fly to Khajuraho, then 45 minutes by road.

There are numerous hotels in Khajuraho. For a more intimate wilderness feel there is the charming Ken River Lodge, which has very comfortable tented suites and some chalets a few minutes from the park gate.

Rajasthan

RANTHAMBHORE NATIONAL PARK
Project Tiger Reserve 392 sq km
(151 square miles)

Ranthambhore has been made famous by the books of Valmik Thapar and the films of Stanley Breedon and Belinda Wright and of Mike Birkhead and his crews. Visitors are attracted by the unforgettable pictures they have seen of tigers sunning themselves in the ruins of the beautiful 1000-year-old fort or hunting sambar along the margins of the park's three lakes. Ranthambhore has

recovered from the ravages of poaching that it suffered a decade ago, but though its tigers are now flourishing, they remain extremely vulnerable. There is little buffer zone, a shortage of water and continual pressure from grazing animals along the perimeter. Its relative proximity to Delhi means that it can sometimes feel a little crowded and the visitor's experience stage-managed. There are fixed routes and large people-carriers travelling along them. Nevertheless, if you stay for a few days you would be unlucky not to see a tiger in lovely surroundings.

Visiting: train from Delhi to Sawai Madhopur (14 km/8½ miles away) takes about four hours. Car from Delhi takes about ten hours. Alternatively, fly to Jaipur, then four hours by road.

There are numerous camps and lodges outside the park, from humble accommodation to a Taj hotel and the very expensive Oberoi establishment.

Karnataka

NAGARAHOLE NATIONAL PARK
643 sq km (248 square miles)

Nagarahole is the northern part of the largest continuous expanse of protected land in southern India. Its southern boundary is separated by the Kabini river from Bandipur National Park and Project Tiger Reserve, which in turn runs into Mudumulai National Park. Together they cover some 1840 sq km (710 square miles). Nagarahole is where Ullas Karanth has conducted his major prey/predator tiger studies and for many years it was ably run by K. M. Chinnappa, one of the best park directors in India. The area, however, has had its ups and downs. There have been recent cases of elephant and tiger poaching and it continues to suffer the depredations of the notorious sandalwood smuggler Veerapan and his gangs. But the forests of teak, rosewood, mathi and sandalwood are very beautiful. They lie in view of the fine mountains of the Western Ghats and still contain a significant tiger population. Bandipur is famous for its dhole, but for tigers, Nagarahole offers the best chances of a sighting. It is also excellent for elephants, especially in the dry season (March to May).

Visiting: from the airport at Bangalore it takes six hours to drive to Nagarahole and seven hours to Bandipur. Train to Mysore (two hours away).

There are forest lodges and camps in all three parks. Nagarahole is the best park to visit. It has the superior Kabini River Lodge at Karapura and the Gateway Tusker Lodge inside the north end of the park. For all accommodation it is best to book early and if possible to avoid weekends and holidays, which can be busy.

Uttaranchal

CORBETT NATIONAL PARK
Project Tiger Reserve 521 sq km
(201 square miles)

India's first national park, this was established as the Hailey National Park in 1936 and renamed in honour of the famous hunter and conservationist Jim Corbett in 1957. It was here, on the banks of the Ramganga river, that Project Tiger was officially launched in 1973. Corbett consists of a wide valley, containing parallel ridges of rugged hills, with the Ramganga river and its associated grasslands winding in from the north and filling the dammed lake in the west. With perhaps in excess of 100 tigers, it is believed to contain one of the half-dozen most important populations in the world. It also has a wide variety of other species, its recorded list totalling some 50 mammals (including wild elephants), 580 birds, 25 reptiles (including the rare gharial crocodile), 110 species of tree and at least 33 types of grass and bamboo. To see a tiger in this grandest of parks is an experience worth living for. Elephant safaris here are particularly peaceful and elephants can be hired at Dikhala in the middle of the park and at Bijrani near the Amdanda Gate.

Visiting: Corbett is some 300 km (186 miles) northeast of Delhi and the drive takes seven hours. Fly to Pantnagar (two to three hours by road). Train to Ramnagar, close to the Amdanda Gate.

There are three gates to the park: Kalagarh in the southwest, Amdanda in the southeast and Dhangarhi in the northeast. The best lodges are strung along the eastern perimeter. Tiger Tops has the very conveniently placed Corbett Lodge near the Amdanda Gate and the Bijrani elephants. Other decent lodges include Corbett Hideaway, Corbett Riverside Resort and Quality Inn.

Uttar Pradesh

DUDHWA NATIONAL PARK
Project Tiger Reserve 490 sq km
(190 square miles)

Dudhwa was established in 1958, originally as a reserve for its sizeable herds of wetland barasingha or swamp deer, largely thanks to

Below: Forest lodge in Dudhwa.

the efforts of one man, the conservationist 'Billy' Arjun Singh. It became a national park in 1977. It is a beautiful park of tall sal forest and wide grasslands, close to the Nepalese border, and shares the characteristics of the terai – the grasslands/low hill-forest ecosytem that stretches along the southern foothills of the Himalayas. I have had exciting experiences with tigers here but numbers are almost certainly lower than the official figures of 90–100 and you have to work a little harder for a sighting here than in Ranthambhore or Bandhavgarh. One problem for the park is that it is a small island of wilderness surrounded by intensive agriculture. When mature, for instance, the kilometres of sugar cane can provide cover for breeding tigresses and their cubs but after harvest the fields are bare and the tigers exposed. Dudhwa has a modest reintroduction programme for Indian rhinoceros and the rare Bengal florican (an Indian bustard) lives in the grasslands.

Visiting: by road from Delhi (eight to nine hours) or Lucknow (six hours). Train to Shahjahanpur (three hours' drive from Dudhwa).

Tiger Haven, 'Billy' Arjun Singh's residence on the southern edge of the park, usually caters for visitors. There is a pleasant forest rest house inside the park.

Assam

KAZIRANGA NATIONAL PARK
430 sq km (167 square miles)

Kaziranga is a little like the Garden of Eden. It lies in the upper floodplain of the great Brahmaputra, which runs along its northern boundary, and its rich alluvial soils support nutritious short-grass meadows, vast elephant-grass jungles, swamps, lakes and riverine forest. Here you can see wonderful mixed herds of wild elephant, buffalo, barasingha, hog deer, wild boar and rhinoceros. According to Ullas Karanth, who conducted a detailed camera-trap survey here in the mid-1990s, it has one of the highest tiger densities of any park in the world, with a population of around 70. These, however, are not clockwork tigers. You have to be lucky to see them and, though I have filmed them here for the BBC, sightings were not frequent. On average I estimate that someone somewhere saw a tiger every five days or so. But Kaziranga

should be visited. Its rhinos have increased from a handful at the end of the nineteenth century to 1200–1400 now. This has been achieved by determined and courageous policing and all the staff, from committed senior officers to barefoot guards, deserve our support and admiration. Nearby moist forests also hold rarities like hoolock gibbon and capped langurs and are full of delightful leeches.

Visiting: fly from Delhi or Calcutta to Gauhati, the capital of Assam (five hours by road) or Jorhat (two hours by road, but flights less reliable). Train to Jakhalabandha (43 km/27 miles).

There are several modest lodges at Kohara but the best place to stay is Wild Grass Lodge a little further east. Elephants can be booked at the Mihimukh Gate at the nearby Central Range. (The park is divided into three separate ranges, West, Central and East).

West Bengal

SUNDARBANS NATIONAL PARK AND WORLD HERITAGE SITE
Project Tiger Reserve 1330 sq km (513 square miles)

Where the three great rivers, the Ganges, Brahmaputra and Meghana, flow into the Bay of Bengal they form a vast delta – a shifting land of streamlets, sands, island forests and mangrove swamps. This is the Sundarbans and it is home to what is

thought to be the second largest contiguous population of tigers in the world, perhaps in excess of 200 animals. The tigers here are shy, unpredictable and dangerous. They really do kill people every year. Visibility is difficult, for the streams twist and turn, the undergrowth is dense and the terrain inaccessible. But tigers are sometimes glimpsed on the river banks – indeed, they have been known to leap into boats – and a visit to the area should be an unforgettable experience. Chital are the main tiger prey. The Sundarbans has already lost its hog deer, barasingha, buffalo and rhinos and this, along with the salinity of the water, may contribute to the tigers' bloodthirsty attitude to humans. The delta also supports estuarine crocodiles and olive ridley turtles.

Visiting: fly to Calcutta, train to Canning, then five hours by country motor launch from the park HQ there to the modest Bengal State Tourist Lodge at Sajnakhali. Transport within the park is by motor launch and small boat. According to the New Delhi-based Environmental Justice Initiative, the Sahara Group is planning a potentially alarming 420-ha (1040-acre) 'ecotourism' project on six Sundarbans islands, incorporating a helipad, airstrip and water sports.

Bangladesh

FIRST CONTACT:

Hasan Mansur, The Guide Tours Ltd, Darpan Complex (1st Floor) Plot 2, Gulshan Circle II, Dhaka 1212

Tel. 880 2 9862205; Fax 880 2 9886984; Email theguide@bangla.net

SUNDARBANS WILDLIFE SANCTUARIES

322 sq km (124 square miles)

The whole delta covers well over 11,000 sq km (4246 square miles) and more than half of it lies in Bangladesh. The formal sanctuaries, however, form only a small area along the far southern tip. They are separated into three reserves: Sundarbans West, Sundarbans South – the largest – and Sundarbans East.

Visiting: fly from Dhaka (Dacca) to Jessore and drive 80 km (50 miles) to the inland port of Mongla. From there eight to nine hours by motor launch to the Forest Department Guest House at Katka.

11	Sundarbans	15	Jigme Dorji
12	Royal Chitwan	16	Jigme Singye
13	Royal Bardia	17	Manas
14	Sukla Phanta	18	Thrumshingla

Nepal

Outside India, Nepal is still the best country in which to look for tigers. It seems to have a relatively stable tiger population of 100–150 animals, three beautiful tiger reserves and the infrastructure to look after visitors. Political turmoil has, in recent years, distracted the army from its protective role, poaching has increased and tourism has suffered. This is a pity because the parks need to be visited.

FIRST CONTACT:

Kristjan Edwards, Tiger Mountain, PO Box 242, Dhapasi, Kathmandu

Tel. 977 1 4361500; Fax 977 1 4361600; Email info@tigermountain.com

ROYAL CHITWAN NATIONAL PARK

932 sq km (360 square miles)

Chitwan is a typical terai park. It lies within sight of the Himalayas and is a land of low hills topped by pines, of sal forest and riverine forests of *Trewia nudiflora*, and of open expanses of nodding elephant grass. It used to be the main hunting preserve of Nepal's kings and its rhinos have traditionally played a central role in the coronation rituals. It was first established as a rhino sanctuary in 1962. Chitwan is bounded by three main rivers – the Rapti to the north, the Narayani to the west and the Reu to the south. It is part of a continuous forest that extends southwards into Valmiki Project Tiger Reserve in India, which makes its core breeding population of around 40 adult tigers a significant one, with the potential to expand. Chitwan was the site of the excellent long-term Smithsonian Tiger Ecology Project and the world's first wild tiger was radio-collared here in 1973. It has also been very well studied by Charles McDougal – chief naturalist at Tiger Tops since 1972 – and his tracking team. Although tigers are never particularly easy to see here, tracks and signs are plentiful. The old days when tigers were baited with live buffaloes and sightings were almost guaranteed are long gone but the tigers are still here, there are 450 rhinos and it is an excellent place to look for sloth bears. The rivers have also been repopulated with gharial (rare freshwater crocodiles) – from a successful breeding project in the park.

Visiting: by road from Kathmandu (five to seven hours) or Pokhara (four to six hours). Ideally, fly to local airstrips at Meghauli or Bharatpur (one hour by road), though the flights don't always run.

Tiger Tops and its lovely tented camp are inside the park, as are Temple Tiger and Chitwan Jungle Lodge. Gaida Wildlife Camp is just outside. All are excellent, with their own elephants and vehicles, but expensive. Much cheaper accommodation to fit all budgets is available in the village of Sauraha. From here you can try to hire elephants from the government elephant camp or even do walking trips into the park

Above: Elephant safari in the terai, Chitwan, Nepal.

with a local guide. I have walked right up to rhinos and sloth bears this way but remember that it is dangerous. Local people are killed by charging rhinos every year.

ROYAL BARDIA NATIONAL PARK

968 sq km (374 square miles)

Bardia is a beautiful park close to the Indian border in southwest Nepal. It has mature forests of sal, open grasslands and savannah-like expanses of mixed woodlands and pasture. It is bounded on its western side by the great Karnali river and its tributary the Geruwa. To float downstream watching ospreys and Gangetic dolphins, spotting wall-creepers and even, if you are lucky, a wild elephant – to have a full cooked lunch on the river bank and then be swept off on an elephant safari to find a tiger – is bliss. I have filmed tigers here, heard and seen them many times and found their tracks everywhere. Bardia is one of my favourite places but this is not Bandhavgarh and I have also had blank visits. Rhinos have

been successfully reintroduced from Chitwan and there are now about 40 here.

Visiting: fly to Nepalganj, then two to three hours by road. The drive from Chitwan takes 12–14 hours.

Tiger Tops have a good lodge near the HQ at Thakurdwara and a lovely tented camp on the banks of the Geruwa/Karnali river. Modest accommodation can usually be found in the nearby villages.

SUKLA PHANTA WILDLIFE RESERVE

155 sq km (60 square miles)

This is a charming little reserve in the far southwest corner of Nepal, right on the border with India. It has hilly forests on its northern side and the rest is moist grasslands and riverine forest watered by the floodplain of the Mahakali river on its western edge. The *phantas*, or grasslands, support plenty of barasingha and they feed a small but healthy population of tigers.

Visiting: the local airstrip at Mahendranagar can be reached from Kathmandu. The drive from Bardia takes about four hours. It can also be reached from India in seven hours by road from Corbett, nine hours from Dudhwa.

There is a tented camp called Silent Safari inside the park.

Bhutan

A route permit is required to travel to places in Bhutan other than the main towns of Paro and Thimphu. This needs to be arranged in advance, so you will need to specify the reasons for your visit.

FIRST CONTACT:

Sunil Rai, Chhundu Travel and Tours, 31 Norzin Lam, PO Box 149, Thimphu
   Tel. 975 2 322592 / 322547;
Fax 975 2 322645;
Email chhundu@druknet.bt

JIGME DORJI NATIONAL PARK

4349 sq km (1679 square miles)

In the northeast corner of Bhutan, this is the largest reserve. It is a mountainous area and altitudes in the park range from subtropical forest with bamboo and rhododendron at 1400 m (4600 feet) to alpine ridges of 7000 m (23,000 feet). The park has takin (a bit like a woolly gnu), blue sheep, red pandas and snow leopards as well as some tigers.

JIGME SINGYE NATIONAL PARK

1723 sq km (665 square miles)

Formerly Black Mountain National park, this area protects the range of hills that separate east and west Bhutan. Comprising virgin alpine and subtropical forest, its southern perimeter borders Royal Manas National

Park, which in turn is connected to the Indian Manas National Park over the border in Assam. This makes up a huge area of contiguous tiger habitat. Unfortunately, Royal Manas is not open to visitors at the moment and the Indian Manas has suffered the depredations of separatist guerrillas, so tiger numbers are uncertain. Jigme Singye remains a good bet, however, and it also has Himalayan black bears, leopards and red pandas.

THRUMSHINGLA NATIONAL PARK

768 sq km (296 square miles)

This smaller park lies further east, between Bumthang and Mongar. It contains temperate forests of chir pine and fir, has red pandas and offers occasional tiger sightings.

Visiting: there are still no commercial lodges in or around the parks. Your tour company should be able to arrange camping facilities for you. The Bhutan Government currently requires each visitor to spend US $240 (£160) per night.

Below: Chitwan grasslands, with the Himalayas visible in the background

Myanmar (Burma)

From 1999 to 2002 the Wildlife Conservation Society and the Myanmar Forest Department conducted a countrywide tiger survey. This was funded by the US Fish and Wildlife Foundation and Exxon Mobile Save the Tiger Fund. Out of 17 priority sites selected and

1 Hukaung Valley	13 Gunung Leuser
2 Htamanthi	14 Seima
3 Myintmoletkat Taung	15 Phnom Bokor
4 Huai Kua Khaeng	16 Nakai Nam Theun
5 Kaeng Krachan	17 Nam Et
6 Khao Yai	18 Phoey Louey
7 Taman Negara	19 Xe Pian
8 Endau-Rompin	20 Dong Ampham
9 Kerinci Seblat	21 Yok Don
10 Way Kambas	22 Srepok River Basin
11 Dangku	23 Bach Ma
12 Bukit Barisan	

surveyed, tigers were recorded by camera traps in three areas.

FIRST CONTACTS:
Thet Zaw Naing, Manager (Ecotourism), Supreme Services Team Tourism Co. Ltd, No. 69 Myaynigone Zay St, Sahchaung Township, Yangon 11111
Tel. 95 1 500500 or 95 1 534490;
Tel./Fax 95 1 501599;
Email SST@mptmail.net.mm

U Saw Tun Khaing, Country Program Co-ordinator, Wildlife Conservation Society, Building C1, 2nd Floor, Aye-Yeik-Mon 1st St, Ward 3, Hlaing Township, Yangon
Tel. 95 1 524893 or 95 1 512984;
Fax 95 1 512838;
Email wcsmm@mptmail.net.mm

HUKAUNG VALLEY WILDLIFE SANCTUARY

6459 sq km (2493 square miles)

In the far northwest of Myanmar, this reserve consists of tropical evergreen and mixed deciduous forest and rattan and bamboo breaks.

HTAMANTHI WILDLIFE SANCTUARY

2150 sq km (830 square miles)

Also in the northwest, a little south of Hukaung valley, the reserve contains tropical evergreen and mixed deciduous forest.

Myintmoletkat Taung

No fixed boundary

This is a large area of tropical rainforest in the midsection of the Taninthayi range in southern Myanmar, east of the town of Pe. It contains the second largest population of tigers in the country but may be off-limits to foreigners.

Visiting: you need a special security permit from the Ministry of Defence to visit remote protected areas in Myanmar. This and accommodation difficulties should be ironed out by dealing with a local tour operator.

Below: Young tigers at play.

Thailand

Thailand's tigers have taken a beating in recent years. But there are still some attractive parks and it is worth being persistent in your efforts to visit them.

FIRST CONTACTS:

Destination Asia (Thailand) Ltd,
TRS. Building, 9th Floor, 21/7 Vibhavadi
Rangsit Road, Chatuchak, Bangkok 10900
Tel. 66 2 272 1458/9; Fax 66 2 272 1460;
Email wanna@destinations-asia.co.th

Neil Challis Wild Watch Thailand 318 Mae
Naam Kwae Rd., Tambon Thamakaam,
Amphur Muang, Kanchanaburi, 71000
Tel./Fax 66 34 512925;
Email neil@wildwatchthailand.com

HUAI KHA KHAENG WILDLIFE SANCTUARY

2574 sq km (994 square miles)

Located in Uthai Thani province, some 300 km (186 miles) northwest of Bangkok, this is part of a World Heritage Site that comprises 12 parks and sanctuaries. To the west and southwest stretch expanses of untouched forest all the way to the Myanmar border and beyond. This whole region is believed to have the potential to hold 100–200 tigers and, though current numbers are probably much lower, it is the best place to look for tigers in Thailand. Unfortunately, a special permit is required to enter and is usually granted only to researchers. You need

to make a good case for wanting to visit.

Visiting: a starting point might be the Country Lake resort at Uthai Thani (approximately 200 km (124 miles) by road from Bangkok).

KAENG KRACHAN NATIONAL PARK

3765 sq km (1453 square miles)

Located west of Bangkok on the Myanmar border, this park contains elephants and primates as well as tigers and is more accessible than Huai Kha Khaeng. Therefore, in practice, it may offer a better chance of seeing something. Special permits are not required, but if you stay overnight in the forest you must report to the park staff and take a guide.

Visiting: three to four hours by road from Bangkok. One hour by road west from the coastal resort of Hua Hin.

Outside the park there is the basic A&B Guesthouse and more comfortable Kaeng Krachan Country Club. To get into tiger country you need to camp in the forest.

KHAO YAI NATIONAL PARK

1945 sq km (750 square miles)

This park, quite close to Bangkok, has the potential to support a small tiger population. It has elephants, sambar, gibbons and sun bears, and raised viewing hides overlooking salt licks.

Visiting: two hours by road northeast of Bangkok.

Malaysia

FIRST CONTACT:

Jabatan Perhilitan, Department of Wildlife
and National Parks, Km 10, Jln Cheras,
56100 Kuala Lumpur
   Tel. 603 90752872

TAMAN NEGARA NATIONAL PARK

4343 sq km (1676 square miles)

Containing 59 per cent of the peninsula's
protected land and with only 13 km (8 miles)
of road and few paths, this is part of a
continuous tract of forest covering 27,469 sq
km (10,737 square miles) extending through
the Belum and Halabala regions to the north
into Thailand. Between 1998 and 2002
Dr Kae Kawanashi surveyed three 120-sq-km
(46-square-mile) sites with camera traps and
concluded the park holds 52–84 adult tigers.
However, her 150 cameras only managed 61
pictures and she never saw a tiger herself.
   Visiting: www.impressions.com.my

ENDAU-ROMPIN NATIONAL PARK

870 sq km (336 square miles)

Straddling the border between the southern
states of Pahang and Johor, this beautiful
park is the Peninsula's second largest and
has had recent confirmed tiger sightings.
   Visiting: Details at www.johorpark.com/
Endau/main.htm, from the Malaysian
Natural History Society, Johor Branch at
www.mnsj.org.my or at www.wildlife.gov.my

Indonesia (Sumatra)

FIRST CONTACTS:

Ketut Sedanartha, Santa Bali Tours and
Travel, Jl. By pass Ngurah Rai No. 70 D,
Sanur, Bali
   Tel. 62 361 286826; Fax 62 361 286825;
Email sedanartha@denpasar.wasantara.
net.id

Sumatran Tiger Project, Dr Ronald Tilson,
Project Director, c/o Minnesota Zoo,
Conservation Office, 13000 Zoo Blvd,
Apple Valley, MN 55124, USA
   Tel. 1 612 431 9267; Fax 1 612 431 9452;
Email r-tilson@mtn.org

Also, for some very basic information: The
Sumatran Tiger Trust, c/o South Lakes Wild
Animal Park, Dalton-in-Furness, Cumbria,
LA15 8JR UK
   Tel. 44 1229 466086;
Email info@tigertrust.info;
Website www.tigertrust.info

KERINCI SEBLAT

13,750 sq km (5307 square miles)

Extending over four provinces in west
central Sumatra, this is the island's biggest
national park. With the Seberida region it
covers more than 16,000 sq km (6176 square
miles). It contains most of the Bukit Barisan
mountain range, including, Gunung Kerinci
(3805 m/12,480 feet), Indonesia's second
highest mountain. It also contains the
highest caldera lake in Southeast Asia and
there are hot springs and waterfalls. The
park is bisected by the Kerinci valley and, as
well as some 50–60 tigers, it supports the
largest population of Sumatran rhinos,
17 species of endemic birds and several
endemic small mammal species. Tigers have
been found from 170 m (558 feet) in the
western lowlands up to altitudes of 2300 m
(7546 feet). Kerinci benefits from an
Integrated Conservation and Development
Project, funded, amongst others, by the
World Bank and involving 134 villages on its
periphery.
   Visiting: there are at least seven decent
hotels in the nearby town of Sungai Penuh.
Further away there are good hotels like the
Carolina Beach Hotel in Padang and
homestays can be arranged in private
houses. To see signs of tiger or even tigers,
however, you need a guide and must be
prepared to camp for at least three nights,
away from the tourist areas of Mount Tujuh
and Mount Kerinci. Researchers are
encouraged and can obtain special research
visas through the Indonesian Academy of
Research (LIPI). Contact Dr Ari Budiman,
Jalan Juanda, 18 Bogor, West Java. Details
on many aspects of the reserve can be found
on www.kerinci.org

WAY KAMBAS NATIONAL PARK

1300 sq km (500 square miles)

In the far southeast corner of Sumatra, in
Lampung Province, this is a fascinating area

of mixed coastal forests. Declared a reserve in 1937, it was heavily logged from 1954–74 and not declared a full national park until 1997. It is mostly flat, under 60 m (197 feet) in altitude. It has swamp forest, lowland rainforest, mangrove and dry-beach forests and extensive grasslands. Apart from its tigers – numbered at 21–36 – it has a very varied mammal list, including gibbons, Malayan tapir and elephants. The park and its tigers are the subject of anti-poaching patrols and habitat and population monitoring under the auspices of the Sumatran Tiger Conservation Programme, a collaborative partnership with the Directorate General of Forest Protection and Nature Conservation. The Sumatran Tiger Trust, based in the Lake District in the UK, also raises funds for research and conservation here and in Bukit Tigapuluk National Park further north.

Visiting: Way Kambas offers some accommodation within the reserve and village housing and hotels exist nearby. It even has an elephant school.

DANGKU PROTECTED AREA

106 sq km (41 square miles)

The whole Tiger Conservation Unit covers some 3431 sq km (1324 square miles) of tropical moist evergreen forest and oil palm in central south Sumatra in the Sumatera region. 21st Century Tiger is financing a conservation project here and radio-collared a tiger in May 2003, a first for Sumatra.

BUKIT BARISAN PROTECTED AREA

4784 sq km (1847 square miles)

A narrow stretch of tropical moist evergreen forest along the spine of the hills parallel to the south west coast in Bengkulu Province, covering 6594 sq km in all. Based on recent photo trap information gathered by WCS, it is estimated to hold 40-50 tigers. This is currently the only accurately censused population in Sumatra.

GUNUNG LEUSER REGION PROTECTED AREA

11,423 sq km (4409 square miles)

Tropical montane forest in Aceh Province in northern Sumatra. A questionnaire-based census in the early 1990s earmarked this as probably the most important area for tigers on the island, supporting around 110 tigers. Unfortunately, this is a lawless region, which is unsafe to visit at the moment. There is civil unrest in the province and armed bandits and illegal loggers in the forests. Researchers are working on orang-utans and elephants but at considerable risk to themselves.

Right: Tiger smelling scent-mark on tree.
Opposite: Hot tiger entering pool to soak.

Cambodia

FIRST CONTACT:
Joe Walston, Deputy Program Director, Wildlife Conservation Society, Cambodia Program, Phnom Penh, IPO Box 1620
Tel. 855 12 954257;
Email jwalston@wcs.org

SEIMA BIODIVERSITY CONSERVATION AREA

1400 sq km (540 square miles)

Situated in the forests of Mondulkiri Province in the far eastern corner of Cambodia, this is the site of an intense WCS/Cambodian government conservation effort. Tiger numbers remain low but since 1999 there has been a recovery programme here to aid the tiger and its prey. Of the areas that still retain tiger populations, this is the most accessible and offers the best chance of seeing signs of tiger, if not actual tigers. It is part of the huge block of habitat, some 52,643 sq km/20,320 square miles (with 13,897 sq km/ 5364 square

miles of it protected), which extends from southern Laos down through eastern Cambodia and over the Vietnam border to include the Yok Don area.

Visiting: contact WCS in advance. The conservation project has started to receive visitors and can guide you (no permit yet required). There are not yet any tourist facilities but WCS can help arrange village-based accommodation and local guides. Their involvement of local people gives work to those who are supportive of conservation and, as Joe Walston of WCS says, helps to 'build the perception that there is a genuine value to wildlife conservation in the area'. This is very worthwhile. If you do visit, you might offer to help the project in any way you can.

PHNOM BOKOR NATIONAL PARK

Protected Area 10,833 sq km
(4181 square miles)

This national park is a large area of moist tropical evergreen forest in southwest Cambodia with considerable potential. With the addition of contiguous but unprotected areas this piece of tiger habitat covers 31,715 sq km (12,241 square miles). 21st Century Tiger is funding a conservation project here. Three new ranger substations are being built, rangers are trained by visiting experts and where patrols are up and running they have successfully reduced poaching and illegal logging. For more details visit www.21stCenturyTiger.org

Laos

FIRST CONTACT:

Roland Eve, Country Director, World Wide Fund for Nature, Lao Program Office, PO Box 7871, Vientiane, Lao PDR.
Tel. 856 21 216080; Fax 856 21 251883
Email roland@laotel.com

George Schaller told me that he recently spent a month hiking through 'tiger terrain' in Laos without finding a single footprint. This is not encouraging. The recent 1999 IUCN status report for the tiger states that it occurs at low densities throughout forested areas. The following areas are considered of particular interest and should be a starting point for any visit. No park sizes available.

NAKAI NAN THEUN NATIONAL BIODIVERSITY CONSERVATION AREA

This area of moist tropical forest is probably the most important place for tigers in Laos and it is where the most recent sightings and camera-trap photographs have been made. The NBCA lies close to the eastern

border with Vietnam but it is part of a much larger stretch of likely tiger habitat covering some 24,626 sq km (9506 square miles) of central Laos, 6830 sq km (2636 square miles) of which lie in protected areas.

NAM ET NBCA AND PHOEY LOUEY NBCA

Both these Conservation Areas are situated in the far northeast, again close to the Vietnam border. They were cited in a 1999 IUCN status report but not included as prime potential habitat by WCS researchers.

XE PIAN NBCA

In the far south, close to the border with Cambodia.

DONG AMPHAM NBCA

In the southeast corner, near the Cambodia/Vietnam border.
Both the above areas are part of a vast tract of good potential tiger habitat extending south over the Cambodian border where most of it lies (see Cambodia, p. 162).

Vietnam

FIRST CONTACT:

Truc Tran, Vidotour, Indochina Travel, 145
Nam Ky Khoi Nghia Street, District 3,
Ho Chi Minh City
   Tel. 84 8 9330457; Fax 84 8 9330470;
Email vidotour@fmail.vnn.vn

The WCS has a very gloomy view of tigers in
Vietnam, a country that has lost 80 per cent
of its forests since 1940. According to Joe
Walston, 'the unfortunate truth is that
Vietnam is no longer important from the
perspective of the species'. It would be
irresponsible to send anyone to Vietnam to
see tigers – but there is no harm in looking
for them! Reports of their existence
continue. Vidotour can help with your
journey, though they know nothing about
tigers.

YOK DON NATIONAL PARK AND GREEN FOREST AND SREPOK RIVER BASIN

Situated in the southwest, on the border
with Cambodia, these areas were one of four
locations that had confirmed tiger sightings
in the mid-1990s (see Cambodia, p. 162).

BACH MA NATURE RESERVE

The area of likely tiger habitat covers 2081
sq km (803 square miles) in the hills of
central Vietnam. Again confirmed tiger signs
during the 1990s.

China

China has become so gloomy about its tigers
that one conservation body has decided to
try to breed Chinese tigers in South Africa!
This presupposes that the 'South China'
tiger is a separate subspecies and that the
exercise is therefore a valid contribution to
conservation. I doubt that it is. In spring
2003 there was great excitement when a
genuine wild Siberian tiger was
photographed at a camera trap inside
China's Hunchun Nature Reserve, in the far
northeast. In the meantime, a tiny
population of wild tigers still exists in
southern China.

FIRST CONTACT:

Mr Wang Zhangqiang, Xishuangbanna
National Nature Reserve, No. 6 North Galan
Road, Jinghong, Yunnan 666100
   Email gtzxsbn@bn.yn.cninfo.net

XISHUANGBANNA NATURE RESERVE

2470 sq km (953 square miles)

A hilly forest area in the western province of
Yunnan. The area has recently been
protected with a hunting ban and the
confiscation of all guns in the prefecture.
According to park staff, wild tigers are now
occurring in the reserve and there are
increasing reports of the loss of domestic
animals along the boundary.

Right: Siberian tiger.

1 Xishuangbanna
2 Sikhote–Alin
3 Lazovsky Zapovednik
4 Ussuriski Zapovednik

Visiting: tourists are accommodated in
local villages and can visit defined areas –
Wild Elephant Valley, Rain Forest Valley, etc.
Serious naturalists should communicate
with the park authorities and may be invited
for a more complete visit. You may be
required to submit an application for
permission to the State Forestry
Administration in Beijing.

Russia

The Russian Far East contains what is probably the largest single contiguous population of tigers in the world. These are the so-called 'Amur' or Siberian tigers, once thought to be a separate race. The last complete census was conducted by the Siberian Tiger Project in 1996 and estimated 435 tigers. These are all found in the 1000-km (621-mile) long stretch of wilderness northeast of Vladivostok in the forested hills of the Primorski Krai and Khabarovski Krai region. Most occur east of the Amur and Ussuri rivers, with a few stragglers crossing westwards over the border into China. They have vast home ranges and are very widely dispersed. Even the largest reserves contain comparatively few tigers and the chances of seeing one are very low. Tracking them, however, and seeing tiger signs in the snow and even on the beaches of the Sea of Japan – where tigers have recently been documented for the first time hunting and killing seals – are very exciting possibilities.

FIRST CONTACTS:

Lucky Tours Co. Ltd, 1 Moskovskaya St, Vladivostok 690106

Tel. 7 4232 449944; Fax 7 4232 491444; Email vladivostok@luckytour.com

Sergei Khokhrjakov, Lazovsky Zapovednik, 56 Centralnaya St, Lazo, Primorsky Region 692890

Tel. 7 42377 91130 / 7 42377 91139;

Fax 7 42377 91137 / 7 42377 91189; Email lazovzap@mail.primorye.ru

SIKHOTE-ALIN BIOSPHERE RESERVE

4,000 sq km (1,544 square miles)

This is the largest of the tiger reserves, lying at the heart of prime tiger habitat, in the middle of the Sikhote-Alin range of hills, where peaks are mostly around 800 m (2624 feet). This is hill-forest dominated by Korean pine mixed with spruce and larch but the temperature and snowfalls of the eastern slopes are moderated by the Sea of Japan and support more southern tree species like Mongolian oak and white birch. The peaks do not present a barrier to tigers but according to Dale Miquelle's researches, the ridges often mark the boundaries of home ranges, so some tigers are mainly cold-forest and others more temperate-forest dwellers. The reserve itself holds 20–25 tigers that have, for the past decade, been the subject of intensive radio-collaring and ecology studies by members of the superb Russian/US co-operative Siberian Tiger Project. Most importantly, the region supports seven species of ungulate: red deer and wild boar being crucial to the tiger's diet, with roe deer, sika deer, thinly dispersed Manchurian moose, alpine musk deer and coastal ghoral (wild goats) playing a secondary role.

Visiting: ten hours by road from Vladivostok. Permits are required from the Reserve Administration (Email sixote@vld.global-one.ru; park director:

Anatoli Astafiev). Guided excursions are conducted into the protected areas. Groups of six or seven can stay nearby in the small towns of Terney, where there is a small hotel, or Plastoon, which is a little further away. Individuals may arrange to stay in a guest house on the edge of the reserve or at the park HQ. The park works with Lucky Tours.

LAZOVSKY ZAPOVEDNIK

1210 sq km (467 square miles)

This reserve, or Zapovednik, lies further south in the Primorski Krai, east of Vladivostok. It currently holds some ten adult tigers and five youngsters.

Visiting: five hours by road from Vladivostok. Lazovsky welcomes small numbers of dedicated visitors, who will receive eight-hour guided excursions. On average 1,000 visitors are received per year.

At the park HQ there is a small hostel and wooden cabins for visitors or researchers with modern office facilities, vehicles, etc. for funded students. Contact the park direct for permits and information.

USSURISKI ZAPOVEDNIK

404 sq km (156 square miles)

A small reserve near Vladivostok.

Visiting: two hours by road from Vladivostock. No official tourist accommodation but Lucky Tours can arrange a visit. The reserve's email address is kaiman@ml.ussuriisk.ru

Acknowledgements

I have been especially helped by the fine work of David Smith, Ullas Karanth, Raghu Chundawat, Charles McDougal, and Dale Miquelle and his colleagues in Siberia. Indeed everyone interested in tigers owes them a debt of gratitude as we do to all the scientists and conservationists mentioned in this book. We should also respect the anonymous forest staff in India and throughout Asia who are working courageously to protect the species. Finally I wish to thank Peter Jackson for his wisdom and support, Julie Tochel and the BBC Books team for their dedication to this project and Vivek Sharma, Tarun Bhati and Liz Drake for working happily with me. In Memoriam: Pradeep Sankhala 1955–2003.

Bibliography

Burton, R. G. 1931. *A Book of Man-Eaters*. London, Hutchinson.

Champion, F. W. 1927. *With a Camera in Tiger-Land*. London, Chatto & Windus.

Champion, F. W. 1933. *The Jungle in Sunlight and Shadow*. London, Chatto & Windus.

Corbett, J. 1944. *The Man-Eaters of Kumaon*. London, Oxford University Press.

Dinerstein, E. & McCracken, G. F. 1990. Endangered greater one-horned rhinoceros carry high levels of genetic variation. *Conservation Biology*, 4, 417–22.

Eardley-Wilmot, S. 1910. *Forest Life and Sport in India*. London, Edward Arnold.

Elton, C. S. 1966 *The Pattern of Animal Communities*. London, Methuen.

Hendrichs, H. 1975. The status of the Tiger *Panthera Tigris* (Linne, 1758) in the Sundarbans Mangrove Forest, (Bay of Bengal). In *Saugetierkunaliche Mittelungen*, 3, 161–99.

Hewett, J. 1938. *Jungle Trails in Northern India*. London, Methuen.

Heptner, V. G. & Sludskii, A. A. 1992. *Mammals of the Soviet Union. Volume 11, part 2, (Carnivora (Hyaenas and Cats)* English Translation, ed. R. S. Hoffman. Washington DC, Smithsonian Institution Libraries and the National Science Foundation.

Jackson, P. 1990. *Endangered Species – Tigers*. London, Apple Press.

Karanth, K. U. 2001. *Tigers*. Grantown-on-Spey, Colin Baxter.

Lack, D. 1943. *The Life of the Robin*. London, Witherby.

van Lawick-Goodall, H. & J. 1970. *Innocent Killers*. London, Collins.

Locke, A. (original 1954 edition is now out of print), 1993. *The Tigers of Trengganu*. Malayan Nature Society, Monograph no. 23.

McDougal, C. 1977. *The Face of the Tiger*. London, Andre Deutsch.

Miquelle, D. G., Smirnov, E. N., Quigley, H. G., Hornocker, M. G., Nikolaev, I. G. & Matyushkin, E. N. 1996. Food habits of Amur tigers in Sikhote-Alin Zapovednik and the Russian Far East, and implications for conservation. *Journal of Wildlife Research*, 1(2), 138–47.

Moss, C. 1976. *Portraits in The Wild*. London, Hamish Hamilton.

Nelson, B. 1986. *Living with Seabirds*. Edinburgh, Edinburgh University Press.

Perry, R. 1964. *The World of the Tiger*. London, Cassell.

Rabinowitz, A.1993. Estimating the Indochinese tiger (*Panther tigris corbetti*) population in Thailand. *Biological Conservation*, 65, 213–17.

Sankhala, K. 1978. *Tiger*. London, Collins.

Schaller, G. 1967. *The Deer and the Tiger*. Chicago, University of Chicago Press.

Schaller, G. 1974. *Golden Shadows, Flying Hooves*. London, Collins.

Seidensticker, J., Christie S. & Jackson P. Eds. 1999. *Riding the Tiger*. Cambridge, Cambridge University Press.

Seidensticker, J. 1996. *Tigers*. Stillwater, Voyager Press.

Smith, J.L.D. 1993. The role of dispersal in structuring the Chitwan tiger population. *Behaviour*, 124, 165–95

Smith, J.L.D. & McDougal, C. 1991. The contribution of variance in lifetime reproduction to effective population size in tigers. *Conservation Biology*, 5, 484–90.

Sunquist, F. & M. 1988. *Tiger Moon*. Chicago, University of Chicago Press.

Thapar, V. 1986. *Tiger: Portrait of a Predator*. London, Collins.

Thapar, V. 1989. *Tigers: The Secret Life*. London, Hamish Hamilton.

Thapar, V. Ed. 2001. *Saving Wild Tigers 1900-2000*. New Delhi, Permanent Black.

Tilson, R.L. & Seal, U.S. 1987. *Tigers of the World*. Park Ridge, Noyes.

Wikenros, K., 2002, Wolf Winter Predation on Moose and Roe Deer in Relation to Pack Size *Examerserbete* No. 75 Grimso, Swedish University of Agricultural Science.

Index

Picture credits

BBC Books would like to thank the
following for providing photographs and
for permission to reproduce copyright
material. While every effort has been
made to trace and acknowledge all
copyright holders, we would like to
apologise for any errors or omissions,
and invite readers to inform us so that
corrections can be made in any future
editions of the book.

Ardea: 15, 16, 20, 70 & 135 Chris
Brunskill, 38 & 62 Jagdeep Rajput, 39 &
118 *bottom* Masahiro Iijima, 40 & 110 C.
McDougal, 76, 127 & 148 Joanna Van
Gruisen; **Corbis:** 123 Yevgeny Kondakov;
Gertrud & Helmut Denzau 106 *top* & 106
bottom; **Nick Garbutt/Indri Images** 52–3
& 98; **Peter Jackson** 34 & 103; **Ullas
Karanth** 35 & 118 *top*; **Stephen Mills** 1, 6,
10 left, 10 right, 11 left, 11 right, 28, 29,
32, 57, 60, 67, 72, 77, 81, 82, 90, 92, 93,
97, 130, 136, 149 top, 150, 155, 158, 159,
162 & 163; **Natural History Picture
Agency:** 33 K. Ghani, 51 Gerard Lacz, 74
Daryl Balfour, 96 Nick Garbutt, 100 Andy
Rouse; **Nature Picture Library:** 143, 145 &
154 Bernard Castelein, 121 Thoswan
Devakul, 149 *bottom* Nick Garbutt, 113 &
124 *top* Ashok Jain, 12–13, 24, 26, 44, 48,
49, 50, 54, 64–65, 66 & 152 E. A.
Kuttapan, 124 *middle*, 124 *bottom* & 129
Vivek Menon, 5 & 17 Pete Oxford, 22 & 75
Anup Shah, 144 David Shale, 117 & 122
Toby Sinclair, 132 Lynn Stone, 114, 141 &
146 Staffan Widstrand; **National
Geographic Image Collection:** 85 Maurice
Hornocker; **Oxford Scientific Films:** 43
Mahipal Singh, 69 Belinda Wright, 108
Vivek Sinha/SAL; **Francois Savigny** 2, 3, 8,
31, 41, 63, 80, 89, 94, 99, 104–5, 109,
116, 133 & 165; **Vivek Sharma** 46 & 160;
Still Pictures: 36 Martin Harvey, 126
Michel Gunther.

BBC Books would also like to thank Iain
Green / Tiger Books (UK), an imprint of
Chevron Publishing Ltd, for the use of their
tiger family tree information from *Wild
Tigers of Bandhavgarh*, 2002.